Text by
**Claire Mackay**

Illustrated by
**Johnny Wales**

# The Toronto Story

Revised Edition

ANNICK PRESS LTD.

TORONTO + NEW YORK + VANCOUVER

Cover and interior design by Irvin Cheung/iCheung Design
Copy-editing by John Sweet

**Annick Press Ltd.**

We acknowledge the support of the Canada Council for the Arts, the Ontario Arts Council, and the Government of Canada through the Book Publishing Industry Development Program (BPIDP) for our publishing activities.

**Cataloguing in Publication Data**

Mackay, Claire, 1930-
     The Toronto story / Claire Mackay ; illustrated by Johnny Wales. -- Rev. ed.

Includes bibliographical references and index.
ISBN 1-55037-763-9

     1. Toronto (Ont.)--History--Juvenile literature.
     I. Wales, Johnny II. Title.

FC3097.33.M35 2002      j971.3'541      C2002-901799-8
F1059.5.T6857M3 2002

The art in this book was rendered in watercolour.
The text was typeset in Times New Roman, Memphis, and Interstate.

**Distributed in Canada by**
Firefly Books Ltd.
3680 Victoria Park Avenue
Willowdale, ON
M2H 3K1

**Published in the U.S.A. by**
Annick Press (U.S.) Ltd.

**Distributed in the U.S.A. by**
Firefly Books (U.S.) Inc.
P.O. Box 1338
Ellicott Station
Buffalo, NY 14205

Printed and bound in Belgium

visit us at: **www.annickpress.com**

To the memory of my mother and father, who cleverly arranged that I should be born and raised in Toronto.

— Claire Mackay

To my late mother Morna, my other late mother Charlotte, and my wife Chieko, ever an inspiration, ever loving and long-suffering all.

— Johnny Wales

# Contents

## From Trees to Tents to Frontier Town

## Growing Pains

## Bright Lights, Big City

## Brighter Lights, Bigger City

| 1793-1814 | 1815-1837 | 1838-1867 | 1868-1904 |
|:---:|:---:|:---:|:---:|
| **05** | **25** | **49** | **63** |

## From the Car to the Crash

## Want, War, Weather— and the Welcome Mat

## Bulldozers, BMWs, and Bag Ladies

## Towards the Millennium ... and Beyond

# Acknowledgements

**The Toronto Story** could never have been told without the help of many people. To name them all would take more space than I've been allotted. Some of them wrote about Toronto, notably Edith Firth, J.M.S. Careless, Bruce West, Donald Jones, William Kilbourn, Mike Filey, Jay Myers, James Lemon, Michael Kluckner, and Frederick Armstrong. My debt to earlier writers Eric Arthur, John Ross Robertson, Henry Scadding, and particularly Elizabeth Simcoe is immense. Some of them found information I needed, especially the librarians at Metro Reference, Northern District, and Dufferin–St. Clair Branch; Nina Gardner of the Bell Telephone Historical Collection in Montreal; Tim Flynn of the Toronto Transit Commission; Bruce Hutchinson of the Ballet Opera House Corporation; Grant Bacchus, a traffic expert who is also my brother; Bill McCreary of the Ministry of Transport; the PR folks at Metro Toronto Convention Centre, the CN Tower, and SkyDome; and the people at Black Creek Pioneer Village.

And some are owed very special thanks: Professor J.M.S. Careless—in whose history class at U of T I sat more years ago than perhaps either of us wish to recall—for his careful reading of the manuscript; Karen Millyard, whose sharp eyes and sensitivity rescued me from error; Johnny Wales, artist, collaborator, and friend, who helped me see things in perspective; my husband Jack, who ran errands, interference, and the whole show for a year or so; and, again and always, my mother, Bernice Bacchus, for her relentless research, for her steadfast encouragement, and for the love of Toronto she instilled in me.

### Acknowledgements for the second edition

Without the research assistance of my friend Pat Hancock, this second edition of *The Toronto Story* would never have materialized. A pack rat par excellence, Pat is superb at finding needles in haystacks, gold in gravel, and delightful particulars in everything. I am deeply grateful.

—Claire Mackay

**In researching the illustrations** for this book, I discovered that rummaging for historical data is much akin to the work of a detective. No all-night stakeouts in darkened cars, eating crumbly doughnuts and drinking cool coffee from a Thermos, but still a seemingly endless round of digging and photocopying, of patching together snippets of clues in an effort to create The Big Picture. Considering the similarity of the two professions, I find myself wondering how the trusty researcher has been so completely ignored in story and song.

I list here the settings of my explorations and adventures, and offer my sincere thanks to all the sleuths who work therein: the City of Toronto Archives; the Metropolitan Toronto Reference Library, specifically the Baldwin Room and the Map Collection Department; the Archives of Ontario; the Thomas Fisher Rare Book Library in the University of Toronto; the Royal Ontario Museum libraries; the Sir William Campbell Foundation; the Toronto Transit Commission; the Metropolitan Toronto Police; the Toronto Public Library, Spadina Branch; and the Art Gallery of Ontario.

I owe special thanks to Mr. Paul Dilse at the City of Toronto Archives for his unfailing patience and help, above and beyond the call of duty; Mr. Al Stencell, The Man To See if you are interested in circuses; Mr. Tim Flynn, editor of the *Coupler* magazine at the TTC; Ms. Edith Firth, for a shot of moral support when I needed it; Carol Martin, our editor; my fellow commiserator Claire Mackay, who wrote this book; and most importantly Chieko, my wife, who is the only reason I was able to complete this book without finishing myself.

—Johnny Wales

The Toronto skyline today. The eight double-page illustrations in this book show how the spot outlined in red has changed over the years.

A Huron fishing camp in the Toronto area before the Europeans arrived. The dwellings are smaller versions of the pole-and-bark longhouses in which the Huron lived permanently near Georgian Bay. The teepee shape near the red tree is not a teepee: it's firewood stacked to dry. With stone axes—the only kind they had—it was just too hard to chop wood into shorter lengths. The creek, one of several that once meandered through Toronto, runs beside present-day Church Street; and the trail along the shore, used by natives for many centuries, is now Front Street. The area inside the red triangle won't look like this for long.

When
Toronto
was
Tundra

# Prologue

This is the story of a city and how it grew: from an unknown and unpeopled place beside an unborn lake to the lively metropolis three million Canadians call home.

**The story begins** 14,000 years ago, in ice and silence. No one was there to break the silence; no one was there to gaze in wonder at the monstrous cliff of blue ice, the glacier that gripped half a continent and soared five times as high as the CN Tower.

But there was life. If, by some magic, you could travel back to that time and look south from the frozen heights, you might see a woolly mammoth lumbering among the few clumps of spindly evergreens; caribou munching on moss and the leathery threads of lichen; or a tiny collared lemming, its white fur nearly invisible in the wind-driven snow. Eighty kilometres (50 miles) further south, where the barren land gave way to forests of spruce and tamarack and white birch, you might glimpse a bull mastodon, his coat of long rusty hair like a fringed rug; a herd of bison whose horns sweep out like wings from their massive heads; shaggy musk oxen nibbling at bark and bud; or a lonely band of horses, soon to vanish, who know neither shoe nor saddle. If you're lucky, you might spot a scarce ground sloth, or the last double-humped camel.

Move forward a thousand years and you might see—tracking the mastodon,

Long before the large-scale immigration to Toronto of people from China and India and Pakistan, Toronto had an Asian connection. The hunter-gatherers known as the Fluted Point People arrived from the south—perhaps where Ohio and Indiana are today—about 9500 BC. Their ancestors had come from Asia many thousands of years before—some say as early as 40,000 BC—when Asia and North America were one. They journeyed down the glacier-free west coast and fanned out south and east, following the animals on which their lives depended.

1

the caribou, the bison, and the horses—frail creatures that run on two legs and wear the skins of other animals over their own, that carry baskets of tough grass and spears with fluted stone points. Humans.

Around 11,000 BC the Big Thaw began. For the fourth time in two million years, the edge of the giant ice sheet softened, thinned, melted, and ran like a thousand floods over the land. The edge was shaped like a hand, with thick finger-like lobes. And, just like a hand that fears to lose its grip, the glacier clawed at the earth as it shrank northwards. It gouged out five holes, five enormous basins. The meltwater rushed to fill them. The Great Lakes were born.

The ice left other gifts: huge webs of rivers, streams, and small lakes; a series of ridges marking the several shorelines of Lake Ontario made by the repeated advance and retreat of the glaciers; vast reservoirs of water just below the surface of the ground; fertile soil conveniently arranged on rolling hills and plains; tons of sand, gravel, and clay; and a wide, sheltered harbour.

The rivers and streams, teeming with salmon and trout, became trading and travel routes. Much later, their power ran electric lights and stoves and toasters.

The ridges became trails, and the

**Fort Rouillé was built by the French in 1751 and burned by the French in 1759.**

trails became highways and streets.

The big underground pools were an endless source of well water for farms and gardens and bathtubs, for drinking and cooking and cleaning.

The soil meant food: everything from cheese to chickens, from strawberries to sausages, from broccoli to burgers.

The sand and gravel and clay were made into roads and bridges and factories and offices and theatres and condos and churches and pizza parlours. And schools.

**As the ice sheet ebbed,** and the land grew green, and the air grew warmer, more and more of these Paleo-Indians, as they are called, hunted and fished and camped on the gentle shore at the head of the great lake into which many rivers emptied. On these rivers travelled copper and silver and cobalt from the northern tribes, sea shells from the peoples of the Atlantic coast, obsidian from the western plains. For uncounted centuries the little lakeshore landing flourished as a natural "place of meeting," or, in the Huron language, "To'ron'to."

It was doubtless a descendant of these hunter-gatherers who, in the seventeenth century, showed it to Étienne Brûlé, the first coureur de bois, a boisterous fellow who changed his wives as often as his shirt—about once a year.

The first North Americans attached fluted stone points like this one to spears as early as 9500 BC.

The 22-year-old Brûlé worked for Champlain at the time, and he was on his way to ask the tribes across the lake for help in fighting the Iroquois. He'd canoed southwest along the Holland River to the upper Humber. There he was stopped by fallen trees and beaver dams. He and twelve Huron companions portaged the remaining 45 kilometres (28 miles)—known as the Toronto Carrying Place—to the shore of Lake Ontario. At twilight on September 9, 1615, Étienne Brûlé arrived in Toronto, the first European to do so.

In the years that followed, the Iroquois chased the Huron away and settled down beside the Humber in a village they named Teiaiagon. Then the Mississauga chased the Iroquois away and used the village as a fishing camp. Then the French moved in and in 1720 built a small trading post. From it they bartered buttons and combs, knives and prunes, looking-glasses and hats, for all the furs they could get their hands on, hijacking cargoes meant for the English whenever they had the chance.

The English, even though they were doing the same thing, didn't like this much, and the French decided they'd better build something bigger and stronger. Fort Toronto, also known as Fort Rouillé, with a baker, a tanner, four cannon, and a few soldiers to fire them, was ready in 1751. A monument in the Exhibition grounds marks where it stood.

It didn't do much good. In 1757 England and France launched a full-scale war, and two years later the French burned the fort rather than let the British take it. England won the war, and in 1788 the British and the Mississauga tribes made a deal known as the Toronto Purchase. The Natives handed over a block of land 23 kilometres (14 miles) across (from Scarborough to Etobicoke Creek) and 45 kilometres (28 miles) deep, including the old portage that Étienne Brûlé had travelled almost 175 years earlier. Interpreter Nathaniel Lines made out the bill. The British got Toronto for £1,700 (about $9,000) and

6 bales Strouds *(heavy cloth)*
4 bales Moltons *(rough coats)*
196 hoes
8 half-barrels of gunpowder
5 boxes of guns
3 cases of shot
10 kegs of ball
24 brass kettles
4 pieces of broadcloth
5 pieces embossed serge
200 pounds of tobacco
47 "carrots" *(carrot-shaped cakes of tobacco)*
432 knives
120 looking-glasses
4 trunks of linen
18 pieces of garter
30 pieces of ribbon
60 plain hats
24 lace hats
2,000 gun flints
432 fish hooks
10 pieces of flowered flannel
160 blankets
1 case barleycorn beads
96 gallons of rum.

It was a steal.

## The Simcoe Connection

There is a holiday in Toronto called Simcoe Day. There is a street in Toronto called Simcoe Street. There is a town called Simcoe. There is a county called Simcoe. There is a lake called Simcoe.

How come? Just who was Simcoe, and why is his name all over the place?

To find out, let's go back a couple of centuries to the afternoon of July 30, 1793. It is hot and bright, and the clean, clear waters of Toronto Bay twinkle in the sun. At the western end of the piece of land we know as Toronto Island—which wasn't an island until 1858—is a 120-ton schooner named the *Mississauga*. At the rail, looking towards their new home, is the Simcoe family.

## 1793 to 1814

## From Trees to Tents to Frontier Town

**John** Graves Simcoe is the father. He's 41 years old and built like a barrel, with a fat face and curly grey hair. He was a soldier—and a good one—from age 18 to 29. After being wounded and imprisoned during the American Revolution, he went back to England, got married, got elected to Parliament, laid out a few roads and gardens on his wife's estate, and lived the life of a country gentleman. Then he was made lieutenant-governor of the new province of Upper Canada. Today, despite the heat, John wears the uniform of his old regiment, the Queen's Rangers. He's here in Toronto to build a fort, just in case the Americans get hungry for land. He also wants to turn the wilderness he sees in front of him into another England—complete with an upper class who will have most of the land and most of the power.

**John's a nice enough fellow**—he loves his wife and children—but he's not an easy man to work for. He's fond of the cat-o'-nine-tails, and once, when a young sentry left his post for five minutes, John had the boy shot while kneeling on his own coffin. His head is full of plans—it always is—and he wants to do everything and go everywhere.

Elizabeth Posthuma Simcoe is the mother. She's 31—but she tells everybody she's 27. She's a tiny woman, no higher than a parking meter, and her brown eyes dart here and there with the jumpy alertness of a chipmunk. Her second name means "after the burial." Her father died before she was born, her mother hours after. A rich orphan, she was raised by her aunt, the wife of Admiral Graves, John's godfather. Elizabeth has too many clothes on: an enormous hat with ribbons flying in the breeze, gloves up to her sharp little elbows, a silk chemise, a whalebone corset, a petticoat, a long, loosely draped dress that looks like a toga, cotton stockings, and leather slippers.

The three youngest Simcoes are on board too. (Four older daughters are back in England.) Sophia, almost four years old, stands beside her mother staring open-mouthed at the landscape, which is mostly trees. Trees, trees, trees,

Everywhere John Simcoe goes, he renames things. He changes Red Pine Fort to Gwillimbury, to honour his wife's family name of Gwillim; Lac La Claie (Fence Lake) to Lake Simcoe, after his father; the La Tranche (Slice) River to the Thames; the St. John's River to the Humber; the Wonscoteonach ("burnt ground") River to the Don; and at high noon on August 26, 1793, to the thunder of a 21-gun salute that makes his small son Francis laugh, Toronto to York, after the Duke of. That one doesn't stick.

Much of what we know about life in early York comes from Elizabeth Simcoe's sketches, letters, and journals. She speaks three languages, draws and paints with great skill, and writes in her diary every day.

as far as you can see—enormous and ancient trees, part of the primeval forest that grew after the ice left: red and white pines 60 metres (200 feet) high and 5 metres (15 feet) around; huge oaks with leaves like dinner plates; fat maples whose syrup and sugar Sophia will soon taste; haughty elms looking down on a grove of flat-topped beech; butternuts battling for a place in the sun; clumps of tall poplars, muttering and fluttering. Most will be gone, chopped down or burned, before another 50 years have passed.

Castle Frank, looking more like Shanty Frank, with Frank and his mom on the porch

**Francis is the well-loved** first son in the family. His name will live for 200 years and more, as a road, a school, and a subway stop, after his parents build a summer house above the Don River and call it Castle Frank. Francis is not quite two, and he looks unhappy in a white dress and lace bonnet. He'll be happier soon: the Ojibwa give him a Native costume and make him a chief.

Six-month-old Katherine, who will die the next spring of "fever"—probably pneumonia—sleeps in her nurse's arms.

John and Elizabeth climb down a rope ladder into a rowboat, and in a few minutes they step out on the shore, just south of where the Exhibition grounds are now. Elizabeth picks out a camping spot, making sure it's not too near the rough huts of the soldiers. John orders more trees chopped down. That night they sleep in what Elizabeth calls their "Canvass House"—which is not your average tent. It has a board floor and plank walls, for one thing. For another, this tent is a famous tent. It once belonged to Captain Cook, the explorer who mapped the coasts of Newfoundland, the Gaspé, and British Columbia, and who had earlier worked for John's father in the navy. After a disagreement about a stolen boat, Cook was killed by Hawaiians on St. Valentine's Day in 1779. All his gear was auctioned off back in England, and John got the tent.

In the months that follow, Elizabeth, Sophia, and Francis do a lot of exploring, on foot, on horseback, and in a boat. They look at a fine grove of oak trees where the town will be built, and where the axes and spades of the Rangers are already busy. They find sweet peas and lily of the valley growing on the peninsula (now the Island). They gaze up at the high cliffs of white sand six and a half kilometres (four miles) east of the townsite, and Elizabeth tells them the family might one day build a house there and call it Scarborough.

**And what do they see** on their rambles? Rattlesnakes, a metre (three and four feet) long (700 are killed near Burlington Bay in 1795); deer, staring unafraid from the dark forest; foxes, rabbits, and squirrels; a bear vanishing into the trees; loons shouting on the bay; a crowd of ducks splashing "in a creek which is to be called the River Don" while red-winged blackbirds sing among the bulrushes along its edge. A bald eagle sits high above on a withered pine, and mosquitoes drone.

They picnic near the half-built Castle Frank, roasting deer meat over an open fire on pointed sticks, the way you cook a hot dog. They gather wintergreen berries, licorice plants, wild grapes, and trilliums. One night, as they count the winks of

**Early rock and roll**

fireflies outside the tent, they hear wolves calling to one another deep in the woods. They eat fried raccoon, which tastes like lamb chops. They eat maple sugar. They eat boiled black squirrel.

Sometimes Elizabeth leaves the children with the maid and goes walking or riding or skating or sleighing with her husband's handsome 22-year-old secretary, Lieutenant Thomas Talbot, who may be the reason she lies about her age. Tom will later control half of southwestern Ontario—St. Thomas and tiny Talbotville Royal nearby are named for him—and die a lonely bachelor in 1853, leaving all his money to his servants.

**The Simcoes camp out** in their tent for the next three years. John bustles about, giving orders, drawing up

In the many streams then running through Toronto, the Simcoes fish for salmon and trout. They watch beavers and otters at play. In the fall they see millions of passenger pigeons, sleek and pink, flying in flocks so large they darken the skies. Soon men will shoot them, net them, and knock them out of the air with sticks until they are gone. In 1914 the last one dies in an Ohio zoo.

plans, laying down roads, making trees disappear—and bickering with his boss, Lord Dorchester, the governor general. Dorchester wants Kingston to be the capital of Upper Canada. Simcoe wants to build a new capital on the Thames and call it either Georgina or London. (Besides, as some people say, Kingston has no land left for him to give away to his friends.) Dorchester orders him to build a fort at Toronto instead. So Simcoe builds a fort—but he also builds a place for the government to meet. Once the government comes to town, there is no turning back: Little York is the centre of power. Because these two men didn't get along, York— later Toronto—becomes the capital city of the province.

More people arrive in the tiny settlement. Most of them are grumpy British government types from Niagara. Leaving their comfortable homes and cozy social

circle for a dot on a crudely drawn map, a raw wilderness that turns to mud in the summer and ice in the winter, where groceries are scarce and mosquitoes are not, isn't their idea of a good time. There are no houses, no churches, no shops, no bridges, no fancy-dress balls, no high teas, no high society. There are no schools either. But John makes them an offer they can't resist: a free acre (0.4-hectare) lot within or near the new town's boundaries (a rectangle formed by what is now Adelaide, Berkeley, Front, and George streets), a huge 100-acre (40-hectare) "park lot" in the forest beyond, and a chance to buy more land at a shilling (24 cents) an acre. It's a give-away.

You can still find the names of those lucky people here and there around Toronto: Russell, Scadding, Willcocks, Jarvis, McGill, Shaw, Macaulay, Denison. Postmaster William Willcocks owned most of the property now bounded by Adelaide, Bay, King, and York. John Scadding, Simcoe's estate manager, had 102 hectares (253 acres) east of the Don River, between the lake and the Danforth. His preacher son Henry lived in a tall, skinny house that still stands, at 6 Trinity Square behind the Eaton Centre. Peter Russell, provincial treasurer and number one man after the Simcoes left, owned a big house near Front and Princess, which

6 Trinity Square, the home of Henry Scadding. From the balcony you once got the best view of the city and harbour.

Land wasn't all Peter Russell owned. Like most of Upper Canada's upper and middle crusts, he also owned slaves. His sister once gave away a young black woman named Amy Pompadour as a present. A few years later, in the *Upper Canada Gazette*, Toronto's first newspaper, Peter Russell placed the following advertisement:

### TO BE SOLD:

A Black Woman named Peggy [Amy's mother], aged 40 years, and a Black Boy, her son, named Jupiter, aged about 15 years … The woman is a tolerable cook and washer-woman, and perfectly understands making soap and candles. The boy is tall and strong for his age, and ... brought up ... as a house servant. They are each of them servants for life.

The price of the woman is $150. For the boy $200, payable in 3 years, with interest from the day of sale… But one-fourth less will be taken for ready money.

his snooty sister Elizabeth named Russell Abbey (look on the map for Abbey Lane); a park lot running north from the corner of Spadina and Queen (Russell Street); and 283 hectares (700 acres) of land farther north (Russell Hill Road, between Eglinton and Dupont). In fact, Russell ended up owning over 30,000 hectares (75,000 acres) of Upper Canada.

**The Simcoes say** goodbye to York in 1796. Elizabeth is "much out of Spirits and crying all Day"; poor little Katherine is buried just east of Dufferin, her gravestone soon lost; Francis, a soldier like his dad, will be killed in Spain before he's 21; Sophia will stay home with her sisters, all

Despite John Simcoe's gifts of free land to early settlers, there is much *not* given away: one-seventh of all land in the province is kept for the Crown, and another one-seventh for the Anglican Church.

eight of them unmarried and bullied by their mother; and Elizabeth will finally die in 1850, outliving John by 44 years, and fibbing about her age until the end.

Little York, by accident more than design, is on its way. The garrison is finished, with storehouses and barracks and even a few second-hand cannon. Its soldiers hang out at a small tavern, now the Wheat Sheaf, on the corner of King and Bathurst.

There's a government wharf in the harbour, and a government mill on the Humber. There's another mill, owned by Isaiah Skinner, on the east bank of the Don, and a road—Mill Road, later Broadview Avenue—to get to it. From that mill, 30 years later, comes some of the first paper made in Ontario.

The Queen's Rangers have hacked out a muddy, stump-filled track that stretches "33 miles and 56 chains" (a chain was 20 metres/66 feet) from what is now Eglinton Avenue all the way to the Holland River. It's called Yonge Street, for England's Secretary of War Sir George Yonge, and

it's pronounced "yawnj." It will grow up to be the longest street in the world. Dundas Street, to link York and London, edges westward. Another road curves five kilometres (three miles) east along the lakeshore to the little bay where Sara Ashbridge and her five children have a farm. And another runs along an old Mississauga Native trail from York to Burlington.

In the town are 40 houses. In the houses, sturdily built of hewn pine logs, live 241 people. A city is born.

## Little Albert

If John Graves Simcoe is the father of Toronto, William Berczy is an uncle. But the name Berczy (pronounced "bear-tzee"), unlike Simcoe, is not all over the place. In fact, it was not until 1975 that

John Simcoe was no big fan of democracy—he called ordinary people "the lower orders"—but he deserves a gold star for one idea: he wanted to abolish slavery. His cronies were shocked and appalled, so John backtracked a bit. The law that finally passed said that people could keep the slaves they had, but they couldn't buy new ones.

Little Albert's livestock had the right stuff. The oxen came in handy, clearing trees off Yonge Street. The pigs came in handy too: for the first few years they ran around the streets of the little village and ate up all the rattlesnakes. Then they turned into pork chops and bacon. Some people think this is why Toronto was first called Hogtown. When the crops failed in 1795, the dogs too came in handy: people ate them.

Toronto took much notice of the man, and even then nobody got carried away: there's a sculptured plaque of his face (and John Simcoe's) hanging in the City Hall, and a stingy triangle of grass beside the Gooderham Building at Wellington and Church called Berczy Park. If you walk by too fast, you'll miss it altogether. Happily, Berczy now has both a school and a library named after him in Unionville, so he is beginning to get his due.

Yet without William Berczy, Toronto wouldn't have got off the ground. Who was he? To begin with, he wasn't even William Berczy. He was Johann Albrecht Ulrich Moll, born in Germany in 1744, one of the six talented children of a rich nobleman. The Molls moved to Vienna when the children were small, and Johann/William studied art and architecture. He was a clever young man, always full of high spirits and risky plans, much like John Simcoe. He loved travel and adventure, and his first job, at age 22, as a spy in Poland, brought him both. When Russia invaded that country, he escaped to Turkey by pretending to be French. In Turkey, to avoid being robbed, he disguised himself as a woman and got a job in the kitchen of the Sultan's harem. A year later, on the way home to Austria, he was kidnapped by Hungarian bandits. He made friends with them and lived in their mountain cave for six months. They called him Berczy, Hungarian for "little Albert" ("Albrecht" is German for "Albert"). William liked the name so much he dropped "Moll" forever. (The "William," however, is a mystery.)

In 1791, after a successful career as a painter in England and Italy, William got into the people-smuggling business. At that time Germans weren't allowed to leave their country, but William secretly gathered 60 families together, tricked the authorities by using an empty ship as a decoy, and sailed for the New World.

**He went first** to the Genesee River Valley in New York state, but there he got into a nasty property fight with a rival immigration agent. In 1794, almost broke and with an American sheriff hot on his trail, Berczy escaped from the United States and arrived at the mouth of the Don River. With him came his German farmers and artisans, a herd of cattle, some sheep and pigs and dogs, and 113 oxen.

John Simcoe had promised Berczy 26,000 hectares (64,000 acres) of land near the Rouge River. William hoped to establish his settlers on some of it and sell off enough of the rest to pay his debts. In return for the land, he agreed to build Yonge Street north to the landing on the Holland River, widening and levelling the original trail laid down by the Rangers.

Bad luck struck again. William got malaria. So did many of his settlers. Some of his workers got hurt on the job.

William and Charlotte Berczy and their German settlers did much for the little pioneer outpost. William himself designed many buildings, including Russell Abbey and St. James' Church. He drew plans for the first real bridge over the Don River, at Dundas Street, a big improvement over the fallen butternut tree with a rope railing used by the Playter family—and which Elizabeth Simcoe was too scared to cross. (Look for Butternut Street, at the end of Playter Crescent, two blocks north of the Danforth.)

And the famine that year didn't help. He missed the deadline on the Yonge Street job, and Simcoe wouldn't give him any more time.

Berczy lost everything. All the undeveloped land along the Rouge and all the Berczy property within York went back to the government. In a 1796 letter to Simcoe, Peter Russell—whose house William had designed—recommended that "the four Lots originally appropriated for Mr. Berczy on Condition that he laid out Yonge Street [by September 15, 1795] ... be sold for whatever sum they may bring ..."

Finally, penniless and bitter after years of wrangling, hundreds of pleading letters, and a stretch in a British debtors' prison, William Berczy, his long-suffering artist wife Charlotte, and their sons William, seven, and Charles, three, left York for Montreal. There he made a living as a painter. His portrait of Mohawk chief Joseph Brant is famous. In 1811, still in debt, he went to New York to try to sell his 1,500-page book *The Statistical Account of Canada*, which he'd been working on for 20 years. He died in New York in 1813, but no one knows how. He may have been murdered. Charlotte later had his coffin dug up; it was filled with rocks. The huge manuscript had vanished. Berczy's death was as strange and dramatic as his life.

The homestead of Elizabeth and Philip Eckardt drawn by their great-great-great grandson

**Charlotte Berczy,** a gifted painter and teacher who is barely mentioned in the history books, kept the settlement running and her family alive when William wasn't around—which was much of the time. The settlers built 72 kilometres (45 miles) of wagon road. They cleared most of the ten-block townsite. They constructed many of those first 40 houses. They turned the narrow, muddy track of Yonge Street into a passable road from Yorkville to Langstaff. Among those settlers were Elizabeth Koepke and Philip Eckardt, the great-great-great-grandparents of the illustrator of this book. Philip, in what is now Markham, oversaw the building of a sawmill and a gristmill, which are remembered today in a winding thoroughfare called German Mills Road. Nearby is German Mills School, where a

grade seven boy named Gordon Korman wrote *This Can't Be Happening at MacDonald Hall.* A little farther north is Berczy Gate, and in Aurora, four blocks east of the troublesome Yonge, is a Berczy Street. We are, at last, saying a small thank you to Little Albert.

## The Russell Regime

With the Simcoes gone, Peter Russell, as President of the Executive Council, took over. Russell was a pompous and painstaking man, an amateur chemist in his spare time, who obeyed all the rules and made sure everybody else did too. He was careful, even stingy, with money. (This may have been because he had had to drop out of college when he couldn't pay his gambling debts.) In a letter to William Osgoode he grumbled, "The Expence of living is most enormous— Beef a shilling a pound, Fowls a Dollar a couple, Flour 7 Dollars a Hundredweight, Laborers 12 shillings a day."

Russell set about to complete Simcoe's plans, pushing the town boundaries north to Lot (now Queen) Street and west to Peter Street, which he named for himself. In 1799 he hired an American, Asa Danforth, to build a road east to the Bay of Quinte. He was enormously pleased with himself over this idea, and wrote to a friend: "I expect the Gratitude of the People will erect a

Russell Abbey, home of Peter Russell, his sister Elizabeth, and their black slaves

Under lieutenant-governors Hunter and Gore, who came after Simcoe, Peter Russell's power declined, along with his health. After a stroke, which was treated with a mustard plaster on the back of his neck and a quart of wine containing crushed deer antler, he died in the fall of 1808—possibly from the treatment.

Statue to my memory for it." He was not nearly so pleased at the cost. Asa, a shrewd Yankee bargainer, held out for $90 a mile, and 200 acres (81 hectares) along the road for each of his 40 workers. Russell had to sell two townships to pay the bill.

Perhaps feeling he'd just been robbed, Russell then had a jail built, at the corner of King and Toronto streets. It was a log hut "of sufficient strength and size to secure 3 separate Prisoners," with "Handcuffs and other Irons for binding gross Offenders, and stocks for punishing those who ... deserve such Chastisement." He didn't bother with beds, blankets, or stoves. And in no time at all he found someone to put in it.

Humphrey Sullivan, an Irish tailor, went on a drinking spree with his pal Michael Flannery, nicknamed "Latin Mike" because he spouted Latin proverbs every two minutes. They soon ran out of money, so Mike forged a cheque for three shillings ninepence (about 90 cents). Humphrey cashed it to buy whisky, of which he'd already had too much. This was a mistake. He was caught, jailed, tried, convicted—and sentenced to hang. Another Irish prisoner, named McKnight, was bribed with a pardon and $100 to do the deed.

**Everybody in town** got dressed up and came to watch, except for Latin Mike, who had long since slipped over the border. McKnight bungled the first two attempts, and finally an exasperated Sullivan said, "McKnight, I hope to goodness you've got the rope all right this time." McKnight did get it all right, and on May 16, 1800, for the theft of less than

1793 to 1814

The town of York's first jail, where Humphrey Sullivan was hanged in 1800 for stealing 90 cents

a dollar, Humphrey Sullivan made history as the first person to be hanged in York.

In the dank cell next to Sullivan was John Small, the clerk of the Executive Council, who had celebrated the turn of the year by shooting Attorney General John White. It seems that Mrs. White thought Mrs. Small had snubbed her during a government meeting. So Mrs. W. complained to Mr. W., who made a few remarks about Mrs. S.'s romantic adventures with a gentleman other than her husband. Mr. S. heard about them and challenged Mr. W. to a duel, the first one in Toronto. Mr. S. was faster on the draw, and on January 3, 1800, Mr. W. bit the dust. Mr. S. was charged with murder,

but acquitted. If he'd stolen a turnip, killed a cow, or worn a disguise in the forest, all punishable by death—what you could call nooseworthy crimes—as late as 1859, he'd have joined Humphrey Sullivan on the gallows. He might even have preferred such a fate: he and his wife were social outcasts for the rest of their lives.

## Students and Storekeepers and Stage Stars

The little town grew slowly but steadily. By 1810, 680 people lived in it, more than half of them children. There were

107 houses, and 27 of these were two-storey. The boisterous frontier village, scorned as "that rough Western upstart" by a jealous Kingston and a smug Niagara, was changing.

Packs of wolves now only rarely carried off sheep from the spacious downtown acres of the rich. Bears seldom attacked horses any more on the street we now call Bay, then known, not surprisingly, as Bear. Although a favourite sport for the townsfolk was getting drunk on a regular basis—taverns outnumbered churches by six to one—York was slowly turning into a law-abiding, even prim place. Most of its leaders, and many ordinary citizens, were British right through to their ramrod backbones, and loyal to the Crown even though it sat on the demented head of George III. They were proud of York's status as the capital of the province and eager to show it off.

There was a lot to brag about.

**There was a weekly** newspaper, the *Upper Canada Gazette*, although it wasn't much more than a propaganda sheet for the government and tended to be late with the news. (It reported the victory of Lord Nelson in the Battle of the Nile five months after the fact.)

There was a church, but only for Anglicans who lived in York. St. James'

Church, a small wooden structure in a rough clearing on King Street where the huge cathedral of the same name is now, opened in 1807. Families bought their own pews, complete with doors and curtains and foot warmers. Whoever paid the most got the front-row seats—and nobody else could sit in them, even when their owners skipped church. When a stranger visited in October of that year, he complained that he "was reduced to the uncomfortable necessity of ... standing as a public spectacle."

There were schools, but they weren't free, and there was no law obliging children to attend. There was also no law saying who could be a teacher: just about anybody—fool, genius, scoundrel, or saint—could set up a school. Yearly fees (no summer holidays, school five and a

The Blue School, which grew up to be Jarvis Collegiate

half days a week) ranged from $18.75 plus room and board for the teacher to $32 and a cord of firewood (a cord is eight feet long, four feet wide, and four feet high—or 2.4 m x 1.2 m x 1.2 m). The children of the wealthy went to Montreal or New York, or they travelled to Cornwall to be taught by the Anglican rector and schoolmaster John Strachan. At first many children learned their letters and numbers from an educated aunt or sister in a private home. One of these, "Old Mrs. Dudley," was briefly famous when her 14-year-old pupil Miss Dunham set herself on fire—by mistake—and sat down on her teacher's books and supplies. No more pencils, no more books. No more Miss W. Dunham either: she died two days later.

Three schools were held in taverns. Another, not quite so exciting, was advertised in the *Gazette* on November 3, 1798:

WILLIAM COOPER BEGS leave to inform his Friends that he intends opening a SCHOOL at his house in George-street, … for the instruction of YOUTH in Reading, Writing, Arethmetic, & English Grammar. Those who chuse to favour him with their Pupils, may rely on the greatest attention being paid to their virtue and morals.

Things were more organized after 1807, when the government passed a law establishing public secondary schools in Upper Canada. The York District School was at first only a shed attached to the house of George Stuart, the minister at St. James' Church, who was renowned for teaching and preaching with his eyes shut. In 1812, John Strachan, the handsome, clever, power-hungry preacher, moved to York and took over as master in a two-storey building painted blue, at the corner of Adelaide and Church streets. His goals were: "to form [sound moral] character ...; to instil religious conviction ...; and to develop a deep affection for the British Monarchy." Strachan later founded Trinity College and, when he became bishop of Toronto, lent his name to an Anglican private school for girls.

People in York could also:
› admire the town's fire engine (horse-drawn, with a hand pump)
› borrow a book from the hundred or so at the library
› send a letter out of town on the government yacht *Toronto*
› watch a prisoner being branded or flogged, and sometimes both
› bargain for a chicken or a cheese or half a sheep in the market at the foot of Jarvis Street, where Berczy's German farmers brought their produce

The citizens of York were horrified by Yankee notions of liberty. They regarded democracy as a rather nasty and impolite disease of rebels and troublemakers that upset the natural order of things. They viewed all churches other than Anglican as heathen, and all threats to their comfort as criminal.

gin, handkerchiefs, inkstands, japanned mugs, knee buckles, licorice balls, muscat raisins, nightcaps, oil, playing cards, quills, razors, spurs, teakettles, uniforms, velvet ribbons, whitewash, Xmas geese, yokes, and Zanzibar ivory combs. Believe it or not, they could also buy jeans, although back then the word meant the cloth from which jeans are made.

› row across the Western Gap to Gibraltar (now Hanlan's) Point to view the first lighthouse on the Great Lakes, still there today
› try on the latest European hats at Quaker Samuel Jackson's on Duke Street
› have lunch (roast veal, mutton, pudding, and beer) in Jordan's Hotel at King and Berkeley
› get their hair or their wigs curled and powdered by "Rock, Hair Dresser from London," in his Ontario Street salon
› if the wind was right, smell Jesse Ketchum's tannery up on Adelaide.

And they could shop till they dropped.

**At Quetton** St. George's brick department store a few blocks east of the apothecary shop, people could buy, direct from New York and London, everything from A to Z: almonds, buttons, candlesticks, dental powder, earrings, fish hooks,

Gibraltar Point lighthouse, the first on the Great Lakes, built in 1808, beamed warnings to ships for 150 years.

Jordan's Hotel, built around 1800 at the corner of King and Yonge streets. It was used for Legislative Assembly meetings after the Yanks burned down half of York.

In the evening, if they still had the strength—and the money!—they went to a show. Travelling theatre groups began to come to York in 1809, and in the following year the people of York enjoyed:

"Philosophical, Mathematical and Curious Experiments"

"Ventriloquism, Songs and Recitations"

"The Celebrated TRAGEDY of *Douglas,* or *The Noble Shepherd*"

"The Comic Farce entitled *The Village Lawyer.*"

Life was good in York. Mrs. Powell, the wife of a prominent judge, wrote to her American brother in 1811: "... every thing here wears a face of improvement, the Country smiles, & we are all sociable together ..."

Less than a year later, her country and his were at war.

## Yankee Go Home!

At sunrise on April 27, 1813, Lieutenant Ely Player of the York militia—whose mother once played cards with Elizabeth Simcoe and whose father made that first shaky bridge over the Don—sees a frightening sight. Out on the bay are 14 American warships, their flags flapping in the strong east wind. On the decks are 1,700 green-uniformed soldiers, with long loaded rifles, under the command of 34-year-old General Zebulon Pike, who yearns to be a hero.

The fleet sails past the lighthouse, where the bleached timbers of the yacht *Toronto,* run aground a year before by a captain named Fish, are piled up like broken bones. As Ely watches, the soldiers crowd into small boats. The wind carries them beyond the garrison to a spot opposite old Fort Toronto, near today's Sunnyside Beach. There, many leap into the icy water to wade ashore, cheering and yelling. Two or three drown on the way. The big ships *President Madison* and *Oneida*, with 42 cannon between them, open fire. Little York, Ely's hometown, is under attack.

**It was the second year** of the War of 1812, "the war that nobody won." The United States had angrily declared war on England the previous June. What they said out loud—very loud—was:

1. England kept kidnapping American sailors, claiming they had deserted from the British navy;

2. England wouldn't let U.S. ships into French ports until they paid a fee—to England;

3. England had given guns to the Shawnee, who promptly attacked an American fort and slaughtered 60 soldiers.

What they didn't say out loud was:

1. It was a good excuse to seize Canada;

2. If they played their cards right, they could get Florida (then owned by Spain, an ally of England) at the same time.

They got Florida. They didn't get Canada. But they certainly tried.

**So there they were** that bright spring morning, on the shore of Lake Ontario, where the new green grass would soon be stained a terrible red. Opposing them were 300 British soldiers (including 120 King's Grenadiers), 200 young Ojibwa warriors, and 300 haphazardly trained boys and men of York, aged 16 to 60, still straggling in from their mills and farms and shops. Many had American relatives, and they weren't crazy about shooting, or being shot by, their cousins.

It was a disaster for both sides. The Battle of York was a confused, noisy, blood-soaked killing ground. The scarlet

After ex-president Thomas Jefferson said, "The capture of Canada is a mere matter of marching," the Americans did just that—and lost four battles in a row. Their bruised pride needed a win, and they thought York would be an easy target. Besides, there was a fine prize to be had. In York harbour was the warship *Isaac Brock*, not quite finished but, with 30 guns, the biggest ship ever. Whoever owned it would control the Great Lakes.

coats of the British made wonderful targets for the Yankee sharpshooters. The storm of grapeshot from the warships was deadly—and everywhere. Grapeshot is just what it sounds like: inside a sphere of thin metal skin lie clusters of cast-iron pellets, like the seeds in a grape. When the sphere explodes, the pellets pierce hearts and heads and bellies with great efficiency.

The militia and a company of British under Captain Aeneas Shaw, for whom Shaw Street was later named, got lost on the way to the beach and wandered around in the woods. Some were picked off by American rifles, but most of the militia concluded it was healthier in another part of town, and disappeared. The Ojibwa sensibly melted back into the forest. Only the King's Grenadiers, brave but stupid, remained in the open, yelling, "Show us our enemy!" The enemy, not quite so stupid, stayed hidden, shooting from behind trees until 90 soldiers fell dead or wounded. Two drowned in the slush-covered deeps of a big pool we now call Grenadier Pond.

**With the fifes and drums** merrily playing "Yankee Doodle," the Americans, led by the glory-seeking Pike, marched to Fort York. They were 400 yards (365 metres) away when the British general Roger Sheaffe, in retreat, gave the dread-

Among those who died in battle was General Zebulon Pike. A rock, hurled through the air like a giant cannonball, ripped a hole in his back and smashed his ribs. He died, not nearly so heroically as he'd hoped, as the American flag rose above Fort York.

ful command to blow up the ammunition dump. Ely Playter dashed inside the fort to get his coat, shouting at the cook to get out. Moments later there was a roar as if the world had split: 500 barrels of gunpowder and a huge store of cartridges, shot, and shells exploded, along with the stone building that housed them. In his diary Ely later wrote:

*... for a few Minutes I was in a Horrid situation, the stone falling thick as Hail & large ones sinking into the very earth. I see Capt. Loring fall with his Horse, & Mr. Sanders also with one leg mashed by a stone ...*

It was a miracle Ely lived. Twenty of his comrades-in-arms were killed or badly hurt. The Americans were in far worse shape: 38 died on the spot, and 222 were wounded. Many of these later died too. Young William Beaumont, a surgeon's mate with the U.S. infantry, got a lot of practice that night. This is what he recorded in his journal:

*A most distressing scene ... nothing but the Groans of the Wounded and agonies of the Dying to be heard. The Surgeons wading in blood, cutting off arms, legs, and trepanning heads [drilling holes into the skull to relieve pressure] ... To hear the poor creatures crying, "Oh, Dear! Oh, Dear! Oh, my God, my God! ... Doctor, Doctor! Do cut off my leg, my arm, my head, to relieve me from my misery! I can't live, I can't live!" would have rent the heart of steel, and shocked the insensibility of the most hardened assassin ... I cut and slashed for 48 hours without food or sleep. My God! Who can think of the shocking scene when his fellow creatures lie mashed and mangled in every part, with a leg, an arm, a head, or a body ground in pieces, without having his heart pained and his blood chill in his veins ...*

**The United States won,** if winning is the right word for the dozens dead, the hundreds mutilated—and the embarrassing escape act by most of the British army. Furthermore, on their way out of York to Kingston, the Brits set fire to the naval storehouses and, helped by Ely Playter, torched the *Isaac Brock*, the very reason York was attacked in the first place.

The Yanks were so upset that they looted and burned half the town. When the rampage ended, the garrison was completely wrecked, most of the government buildings were ablaze, and the shops along King Street were nearly emptied, especially of wine and rum and brandy. Private homes were pillaged of everything from carpets to cutlery, saddles to silver toast racks. Mrs. Givins, whose officer-husband had led the Ojibwa into battle, was robbed of all her worldly goods, including the clothes of her seven children. General Sheaffe, who left in a hurry, lost his solid gold snuff box. From his hiding place in the woods Ely Playter watched as American soldiers smashed through the door of his Yonge Street farmhouse and made off with his sword, his razors, his powder horn, his boots, and his cloak.

The Americans stole all the books from the tiny library. They stole the

In 1814, York got revenge on the Americans by setting fire to the U.S. president's mansion in Washington. The charred walls were later covered with white-wash—and ever since it's been called the White House.

small carved wooden mace from the Parliament Buildings. (We got it back at last in 1934, and you can now see it at Fort York.) They even stole the brand-new fire engine Little York was so proud of, and which was badly needed two days later when the Parliament Buildings went up in flames. To this day nobody is sure who did it, but a gang of American sailors was seen loitering nearby.

And, in a search for hidden gold, American soldiers ransacked the empty log house on the hill, Castle Frank. It was a year almost to the day since the laughing boy for whom it was named died on a Spanish battlefield, in the shadow of another ruined castle, fighting the same foolish war.

When the Yanks looted St. James' Church, however, they went too far.

**Enter John Strachan,** in a flowing black cloak and black boots, tall in the saddle, awesome in his righteous wrath, looking a bit like Batman. He demanded that the looting stop, the terms of surrender be observed immediately, the prisoners be released on their honour, and all the damage be paid for. He scolded the American general Dearborn as if he were a small boy breaking windows with a slingshot. Poor Dearborn, who had been throwing up all week from seasickness, was so dumbfounded he agreed.

With a single bold stroke John Strachan became—and for the next 25 years remained—the most powerful man in York.

## For Richer, For Poorer ...

The war was cruel and senseless, and it solved nothing. But the little town wasn't too badly hurt. Only five men of York had fallen, and only five were wounded. A few buildings were gone, and some houses robbed. As they began to restore their town, the people of York, for perhaps the first time, felt united. They had literally come through fire together. They had fought and suffered and survived together. They were proud of themselves, and proud of their community. They set about making it grow.

# 1815 to 1837
# Growing Pains

William Cooper's wharf, between Fort York to the west and the town centre a few blocks east, is where the action is: the lake is the fastest, easiest, and cheapest way to move people and goods. The stockade with the flag is the town's first jail, but it also serves as a refuge for the townspeople in case of attack. The white house with the green roof belongs to Chief Justice Thomas Scott. In his backyard, as in most backyards, is a fruit and vegetable garden; people grow much of their own food even in the town. Beside Judge Scott's place, a party of settlers is clearing the land by pulling up tree stumps and moving rocks. The old trail along the shore has changed: the European settlers have widened it for their wagons.

**And** in the next twenty years it did just that. The population, helped along by new Scottish and Irish and English immigrants, jumped from 720 to 9,250, and on market days King Street was solid with shoppers. The 20 stores of 1814 became 100 by 1834, and 117 houses grew to 1,014, nearly half of them two-storey. The town even got its first "office block": at the corner of King and York streets rose the Chewett Buildings, which held apartments, offices, stores, and the British Coffee House, a popular hangout for the rich. Churches, schools, hotels, and taverns (there were 60 places to drink by 1830) sprang up everywhere, spilling over the Old Town boundary of Jarvis Street—where rival gangs of boys hurled stones, punches, and curses at each other—into the section called New Town, which extended north to Lot (Queen) Street and west to Peter Street.

**The first cab** in York was a gorgeous red-and-yellow one-horse carriage named "The City," owned by Thornton Blackburn, one of the growing number of York's black citizens who had found freedom in Canada via the "underground railway." He and his fellow cabbies often waited under the big blue-and-gold arch of the town's first full-time theatre, the Royal on King Street, or near the Steamboat Hotel, which once featured "The Extraordinary Exhibition of the Industrious Fleas from England."

Stagecoaches full of mail and people travelled between York and Kingston by 1817, and ten years later there was a regular mail delivery from Hamilton and points west. There were no postage stamps yet: the first Canadian stamp, a red square with a beaver on it, wasn't printed until 1851 (see page 59), and cost three pence (six cents). In mint (unused) condition it's now worth $20,000. There were no envelopes either: you folded your letter so that the four corners

Thornton Blackburn driving his cab "The City." The red and yellow of his vehicle became the colours of the TTC streetcars and buses.

York got so crowded that it soon had its first traffic laws. Parked vehicles had to be "arranged along the sides [of the streets] in a regular manner on penalty of five shillings." Nobody could "gallop or ride or drive a horse at an unreasonable rate of speed," or leave a "Waggon, Cart, or Carriage ... standing in the street for more than 24 hours." More laws were passed when cabs—short for "cabriolets," horse-drawn carriages for hire—appeared around 1834. A driver was forbidden to "wantonly snap or flourish his whip" or use "abusive, obscene, or violent language."

touched in the middle, as if you were making a paper airplane, and sealed the spot with hot wax. Then you gave some money—a dollar for a letter to England, 66 cents to Halifax, 18 cents to Kingston—to the postmaster in his little log hut on Frederick Street. You picked up your mail there, too. Home delivery didn't start till 1847, when Toronto's first letter carrier, John McCloskey, brought your letters right to your door. He was paid a penny (two cents) for each piece of mail.

One of the first men to use steam power was James Worts, who built a gristmill on the bay near the Don River with his brother-in-law William Gooderham. They let the farmers pay them with extra grain, and finally they

had so much that they decided to make whisky out of it. Gooderham & Worts became the second biggest whisky-maker in the world. Unfortunately, neither James nor his wife were around to enjoy the success: James drowned himself in the well of the mill when his young wife died in childbirth. Such deaths were shockingly common. While Canadian figures are scarce, hospital studies in other countries suggest that one woman in six died giving birth, which amounts to a plague.

**Businessmen began** to specialize—to make or sell only one item. Peter Freeland built his soap factory at Yonge

The town of York's first post office, at King and Frederick streets

and Front and really cleaned up. Fred Dutcher's Plough Manufactory at King and Yonge had 80 workers, melted a ton of iron a day, and turned over a lot of money. The Ridout Brothers Hardware Store nailed down hundreds of customers and hammered out a good living. There were shops that sold only dishes, or drapery, or drugs. There were printers, booksellers, and stationers. There was a steam engine factory, a leather manufacturer, and a carriage works.

And there were even a few businesswomen—with brave hearts and bold spirits—who set up enterprises on their own. They were lacemakers, seamstresses, midwives (safer by far than doctors), practical nurses, spinners, weavers. Several women of the middle and upper classes founded girls' schools. Others, such as Sara Ashbridge and Elizabeth Russell, managed their own estates and farms.

A rare few made money by writing, no easy task then as now. Anna Jameson was one of them. Anna came to Toronto in 1836, when she was 42, to join her husband, the Attorney General. She didn't like the city, or the people who ran it, and she said so:

*[The city] is like a fourth or fifth-rate provincial town ... We have here a petty colonial oligarchy, a self-*

At the mouth of the Don River stands James Worts's mill, a year after he drowned in its well.

*constituted aristocracy, based upon nothing real nor upon anything imaginary. The cold narrow minds, the confined ideas, the by-gone prejudices ... are hardly conceivable ...*

She looked around at the felled trees and the rotting stumps and wrote:

*A Canadian settler hates a tree, regards it as his natural enemy, as something to be destroyed, eradicated, annihilated by all and any means.*

Anna stayed only eight months—probably to the great relief of many—but they were action-packed. Tough-minded, curious, and awesomely intrepid, she travelled in a small boat with voyageurs to the wilderness post of Sault Ste.

By 1826 there were five steamboats churning up the waters of Lake Ontario. One of them, the *Canada*, was built at the mouth of the Rouge River, then towed to York to get her engine and boiler. Her first trip, from York to Niagara, took four hours. Steam also came to the new factories and foundries, putting the horses out of work.

Marie. She was the first European woman to shoot the rapids of the St. Mary's River, a courageous deed that prompted the Ojibwa to adopt her as Wah'sah'ge'wah'no'qua, "the woman of the foam." She took part in the yearly Native assembly on "Manitoolin" Island, and then made her way by canoe and portage back to Toronto. She left a tangy tale of her Canadian sojourn in *Winter Studies and Summer Rambles in Canada*. She left her husband too, an action unheard of at the time, but not before she got a separation agreement and a generous allowance out of him—also unheard of at the time. Then, sadly for us, she left Canada, never to return. Her husband, not surprisingly, was "much displeased" with her book.

**With all the new stores** and factories and businesses, York was a boom town. It was time for a bank. In 1822 the Bank of Upper Canada opened its ele-gant doors near King and Frederick, where part of George Brown College is today. John Strachan helped set it up. He worked behind the scenes, pulling strings like a puppeteer, making deals like a snake-oil salesman, ensuring that his cronies were in charge. In a letter to John Macaulay he says that the bank will make a mint of money for them, tells him how to get the job of director, and ends with these words: "I write confidentially nor need anyone know I have addressed you on the subject."

The rich got richer—and built mansions.

D'Arcy Boulton, at one time the wealthiest man in Upper Canada, built The Grange, now part of the Art Gallery of Ontario.

Dr. William Warren Baldwin, who had tried to cure Peter Russell with the crushed deer antler, built "a commodious house in the Country" called Spadina. It

The money system in early York was a mess. There were British pounds, Halifax pounds (worth less than the British), American eagles ($10 gold coins), Spanish dollars, French francs, odd coins from the Caribbean and Africa, and bits of paper with unreadable numbers. Most people gave up and traded goods instead.

was then pronounced "Spadeena," from the Native *ishapadenah*, meaning "hill." He cut a swath through the chestnut trees to the south—a swath later known as Spadina Road—so he could "see the vessells passing up and down the bay."

Two years later, in 1821, Dr. Baldwin welcomed a neighbour to the west. Joseph Wells, who had fought beside young Francis Simcoe in Spain, built a two-and-a-half-storey stone house called Davenport.

Rosedale, overlooking the ravine north of Yorkville, was built as a country house by Stephen Jarvis and inherited by his son, Sheriff William Jarvis. The Sheriff, a real party animal, threw terrific fancy-dress balls, but his guests had to slog through the mud of Yonge Street and pay at the Bloor Street tollgate—one of many around the town—to get there. The mansion itself is long gone, but the coach house still stands near Rosedale Road and Cluny Drive.

William Allan, the bank's first president, was a storekeeper who had made a fortune in the war. He already had a big house on Front Street, but he built a bigger one out in the suburbs. He called it Moss Park. Later on, his son George, whose house The Home Wood stood where Wellesley Hospital is today, gave the city 4 hectares (10 acres) for its first park, now known as Allan Gardens.

John Strachan, the poor son of a quarryman, who had vowed never to be poor again, built himself a palace. Set smack in the centre of the block bounded by Front, York, Wellington, and Simcoe, it was a magnificent brick edifice of many rooms, many chimneys, and many windows of leaded glass. It cost him £6,000, about $30,000, a fortune in 1818. When his brother James, visiting from Scotland, saw it, he said: "Jock, Jock, ye've a hoosie like a palace ... Eh mon, I hope it's a' come by honest." There is no record of John's reply.

**But one rich** man—Jesse Ketchum—continued to live simply in a plain wooden house (in front of which was the first sidewalk in York, made of bark) beside his tannery on Adelaide Street. Jesse had

John Howard, the architect and city surveyor who designed the Chewett Block, the Insane Asylum at 999 Queen Street West, and many other buildings, built a cottage he called Colborne Lodge (in honour of the lieutenant-governor) on his property in High Park. The Lodge was famous for its indoor bathroom—one of the first in Toronto—even though it was hard to find: its door was covered with the same wallpaper as the walls and kept closed when the Howards had guests. Bathrooms were never talked about in polite society.

made money in the war too—but he gave most of it away. He gave it to churches and to charities; he gave it to buy books; he gave it to set up free schools for poor children; he gave it to anybody in need. He also bought some land near the village of Yorkville and turned it into a children's park. In the middle of that long-ago park now stands Jesse Ketchum School, a fitting monument to this gentle, homely, kindly man—who couldn't read and write until he was 40. More than a century later, through the doors of that school came a nervous eight-year-old named Jean Little, whose books are now known to children around the world.

The poor, on the other hand, did not get richer. They built tiny log cabins, and shacks, and shanties, and small frame houses. They had windows of oiled paper or rags, mattresses of elm bark or straw, a few homemade chairs and a table, candles of melted fat, and wooden dishes. The women of the family made all the clothes by hand; the sewing machine didn't exist. Nor did stoves until the late 1820s, so all cooking was done—by the women, of course—in a big open fireplace.

**In fact,** women worked all the time. The life of Elizabeth Fisher Stong is typical. Born in 1798, Elizabeth inherited a huge area of uncleared land. At 18 she married Daniel Stong, and her land became his; married women couldn't own property. On that land there later rose the many buildings of York University, Stong College among them. And the Stong homestead, hacked out of the bush, is now the main attraction at Black Creek Pioneer Village. Beside its small church is Elizabeth's grave: she died in 1885, at age 87.

How she lived that long is a wonder. Here's a list of some—not all—of the things Elizabeth did in an average year:

> have a baby
> milk the cows, churn the butter, and make the cheese
> feed the chickens and gather their eggs
> bake the bread
> plant, weed, hoe, and harvest the vegetable garden
> dry and preserve the vegetables and fruits
> make soap from what was politely termed "chamber lye" (urine)
> gather herbs to make medicines
> soak, soften, and spin flax to make clothes and sheets
> wash, dye, card, and spin wool, then knit it into mitts, socks, and scarves
> wash clothes, wash sheets, wash handmade quilts and towels, all by hand
> iron all the stuff she washed

> cook and clean all day every day

> have another baby

Just reading it makes you want to lie down and have a nap.

But endless as her work was, at least Elizabeth, living in what was then the country, had space to move around in and clean air to breathe. In the city, many women were not as lucky. The poor lived in "Macaulaytown," a near-slum northwest of Queen and Yonge, subdivided into tiny lots by the Macaulay family; they crowded together along the lower Humber; they huddled ten to a room in small houses beside the warehouses on the waterfront; they breathed the foul air of the mosquito-infested lands near the Don River.

## In Sickness and in Health

And just like William Berczy, who had camped near the swamp years before, many of them got sick. Some may have been bitten by mosquitoes that carry malaria, but nobody blamed the mosquitoes. Most people, including the few doctors in town, blamed the "miasma," the smelly vapours that hovered above the swamp like an evil fog. They were wrong: it wasn't the smell that made people sick, it was the stuff that made the smell.

It was garbage. All kinds of garbage, in colourful stages of decay. Food scraps,

Nobody came around to collect the garbage. People just threw it in the roads, or in the woods north of Queen, or in the stinking ditches around the town, or in the Don or the Humber, or into the lake itself. Forty years after Elizabeth Simcoe delighted in the "beautifully clear & transparent" waters of Toronto Bay, another writer, Francis Collins, called those waters "carrion-broth."

factory rubbish (tree bark, sawdust, metal shavings, coal dust, cow and pig and fish guts), human waste, dead animals—all of it a giant cafeteria for maggots, flies, rats, and bacteria by the billion. (No empty cans, though: canned food wasn't at the local grocery till around 1895. The can itself, called a canister, was invented by Peter Durand in 1808. It was made of iron, and weighed a pound. The British navy tried it in the War of 1812, but because there was no can opener until 1858, a sailor had to use a knife, or a bayonet, or sometimes a rifle, to liberate his lunch.)

**Francis Collins** was the owner of the *Canadian Freeman*, one of the seven newspapers in the York of the 1830s, and he was a man who spoke his mind, a habit that often got him into trouble. He went to jail twice for libel, once calling

Attorney General John Beverley Robinson "a native malignancy." Of the lake he wrote:

*It is really astonishing how the magistrates can allow the horrible nuisance which now appears on the face of [the] Bay. All the filth of the town—dead horses, dogs, cats, manure, etc. heaped up together on the ice, to drop down, in a few days, into the water which is used by almost all the inhabitants on the Bay shore. If they have no regard for the health of their fellow-beings, are they not afraid to poison the fish that supply their own tables?*

And five weeks later, when York at last appointed a medical officer, he wrote:

*... the cleanliness of the Town, or rather its filthiness, ought to engage the first attention of this officer. Stagnant pools of water, green as a leek, and emitting deadly exhalations, are ... in every corner of the town—yards and cellars send forth a stench ... from rotten vegetables sufficient almost of itself to produce a plague—and the state of the Bay, from which a large portion of the inhabitants are supplied with water, is horrible ...*

All his nagging paid off. The town soon hired its first garbagemen, who were called scavengers, and built drains in the poorest and dirtiest neighbourhoods—but not before York was hit with a raging epidemic of cholera.

Cholera is not nice. It's been around forever, and it still kills more than 10,000 people a year. People catch it from infected food or water, things York had plenty of. It starts with terrible diarrhea and hours of vomiting. Then all the muscles of the body cramp and the skin turns blue because it's out of oxygen. Without treatment, half the people who get it die, sometimes within six hours.

**Every now** and then cholera spreads through a large part of the world. When it does, it's called a pandemic. This is what happened in 1831. Carried by travellers from India across Europe to England and Ireland, killing millions on the way, it stowed away inside some immigrants and sailed to North America in June 1832. Three months later there were close to 6,000 corpses, 237 of them in York. There was hardly room to bury them all, and Francis Collins began to nag again:

*The most dangerous nuisance in York ... is the burying-ground of the English Church. It is situated ...*

*where no cemetery ought to be, in the very centre of the town, and so crowded ... that they had to bury the cholera sufferers in a swampy corner where it is revolting to see remains of human beings deposited in mud and dirty water! Such low, wet soil, it will crack open in summer ... and who can say what pestilence and death may be exhaled from such chinks?... Bodies were interred ... [secretly] in the dark, and so carelessly that in walking across the cemetery ... this spring, we saw some of the graves ... down to the coffin lids ... The cholera-swamp ought to be covered six inches deep with lime ...*

Now, of course, we know how to prevent cholera. We know how to treat it, and we know quite a lot about germs. But back then nobody knew a germ from a gerbil. A common treatment for cholera—and just about everything else—was a syrupy medicine laced with alcohol or opium; some patients probably died happy as a result. Another popular potion was a mixture of two tablespoons of charcoal, two of hog fat, and two of maple sugar, given at half-hour intervals.

Many people relied on home remedies, or medical lore learned from the Native people. When Elizabeth Russell had heart trouble in 1811 and swelled up

Doctors used to put bloodsuckers, or leeches, captured from the local swamp, on a sick person's skin to suck out whatever was wrong. The treatment cost 60 cents, and it was supposed to cure people of headaches, black eyes, strokes, pimples, insanity, whooping cough, and a dozen other diseases. It undoubtedly cured some people of doctors.

like a balloon, she drank tea made from foxglove, a wildflower containing a chemical called digitalis, and used for centuries by the Natives. Her heartbeat settled down right away, and after Dr. Baldwin stuck a tube in her and drained off 18 pints (8.5 litres) of fluid, she lived another ten years.

**In 1834** a second and far worse cholera epidemic invaded York. It killed 750 people, nearly a tenth of the population. Most of them were new immigrants. But one who died was the cranky, crusading newspaperman, Toronto's first environmentalist, Francis Collins.

As the plague spread, a law was passed saying that anybody "infected by, or tainted with pestilential matter" had to go to the hospital. This was a two-storey building on King Street West near Peter Street. It was built in 1820 and later became the Toronto General Hospital. Nobody wanted to go. It was a bad place to be if you were sick. It wasn't too clean, of course; nothing was. Dirt was a fact of life—and of death. There were no bathtubs in the hospital until 1870. If the patients—or the doctors—wanted a bath, they had to use the laundry tubs in the cellar.

Next to the tubs lived the nurses, fighting for space with the armies of rats and beetles, and sometimes throwing drunken parties that shocked the town. Nurses were mostly farm girls with strong backs and strong stomachs, experts in cow-dung poultices and calf-birthing, and the only people who would put up with the disgusting work and the disgusting pay—about six dollars a month. Training for nurses wasn't even thought of until 1881.

**Surgery was about** as popular as being burnt at the stake. There were no anaesthetics. A doctor poured brandy down his patient's throat or held a pillow over her face until she passed out. "Old Tom," the janitor at the hospital, toughed out two operations with his eyes wide open. Wounded in 1805 during the Battle of Trafalgar, Tom had a leg sawn off while biting on—and possibly through—a nail. After he got the hospital job, Tom spent most of his time sitting under a tree

**The "Death Cart" carried the victims of cholera to their graves.**

The notion of washing his hands or his instruments never crossed a doctor's mind. He carried his stethoscope in his tall black hat, and his knives and lances in a little pocket of his coattails. During an operation he often held his scalpel in his mouth and wiped his hands on a bloody apron, like a butcher's.

smoking a pipe. Then he got cancer of the tongue. He couldn't bite a nail this time, and he refused the brandy and the pillow. The doctor clamped a metal twisting device on Old Tom's tongue and then tightened it till the tongue dropped off. The next day Tom was back under the tree smoking his pipe.

By 1832 the town even had a part-time dentist. Mr. Wood opened an office at 233 King Street East and put an ad in the paper promising "a constant supply of French Enamel Teeth, which have ... a reputation for durability, strength, and beauty," which he would "fasten with the latest improved methods, from one to a Full Sett."

## Rise of the Rebel

Two men, each powerful in his own way, each the sworn enemy of the other, and each a profound influence on the city, the province, and finally the country, are seen on the streets of York during the cholera epidemics. When the rich flee to their country homes north of Queen, when others bar their doors to the dying, and shun the sick, and burn tar and sulphur to fend off the evil vapours, two men stay to help. Day after day they drive the covered "Death Cart" through the muddy ruts and potholes, stopping to pick up corpses from the tumbledown shacks of the poor, from the doorways of taverns and churches, from the littered shore of the bay, from the stinking ditches.

And they cannot be more different.

One is John Strachan, tall, handsome, wealthy, dignified. John is an archdeacon now, part of the ruling class, a member of the Executive and Legislative councils. He is the maker of rich men's fortunes and the moulder of their sons' beliefs. He is the big wheel in the back room who runs Upper Canada, a self-proclaimed aristocrat who thinks the universe is unfolding quite pleasantly, just as he and God planned it.

The other is William Lyon Mackenzie, short (to reach the dinner table he needs a thick dictionary on his chair), always down to his last farthing, with eyes of blue lightning, a jaw like a tombstone, a nose like an axe—and a tongue like a flame-thrower. His hands and feet are never still, and his huge head is bald as a bowl, the result of a childhood fever. Where his hair should be is—off and on—an orange wig, uncombed and crooked, a nest built by a slovenly bird.

**Mackenzie is** an eloquent speaker and an elegant writer: it is he who dubs the ruling elite, with its intricate links of blood and marriage, "The Family Compact," a phrase found in every Canadian history book. He is a smart man, a passionate man, a man faithful to

**Mackenzie blows his top – and throws his top.**

his friends and to his ideals, an exuberant father to his many children (14 are born; 7 live) when he has the time. But he is also an impatient man, quick to anger and quicker to attack, a revolutionary who thinks the universe, especially the speck called York, is unfolding very badly indeed, and needs to be fixed. By him.

Lyon—for so he was called (along with rascal, slanderer, ruffian, disgrace, traitor, madman, and vermin; or, depending on who was talking, patriot, liberator, democrat, reformer, and saviour)—was born in 1795 near Dundee, Scotland. At age 27 his father, Daniel, a weaver who never had a penny, married Lyon's mother, Elizabeth. She was 45, a doll-sized woman with a twitchy face that didn't know how to smile. Three weeks after Lyon was born, Daniel died. Proud, poor, and fiercely religious, Elizabeth refused help from everyone, once weaving and selling a Mackenzie tartan to get a cup of barley meal for Lyon's breakfast.

Lyon was a brain at the local parish school, but he was also the class clown. He drew caricatures of his teachers, and mimicked them in front of the other children. He got whipped about once a week, and he grinned through it all.

At 19, after a couple of years as an office clerk, Lyon opened his own general store and lending library, but times were hard after the War of 1812 and he went broke. He wandered through England and then to Paris, where he got hooked on gambling and a few other things he never told his mother about. Finally, a friend suggested they seek their fortunes in the New World.

**So, in 1820,** Mackenzie landed in Upper Canada. He ran a drugstore in Dundas for a while, making $500 a month in profits. He married a young woman named Isobel, who had come from Scotland with his mother. In 1824, in his usual restless and impulsive way, he sold his share of the business, moved to Queenston, and started a newspaper.

But York was where the action was. A year later, so was William Lyon Mackenzie, with his wife, his children, his mother, his printing press, and his wig—and the ideas that would ignite a rebellion.

The town has never been the same.

## The Type Riot

From Lyon's printing press on Palace Street came editorials that just about blistered the paint on John Strachan's mansion five blocks west. Lyon said the big shots were thieves, and their hangers-on "funguses." He said Strachan, the saintly hero of York, was a demon, a hypocrite, and "the Governor's jackal." He said the female ancestors of Attorney General John Beverley Robinson, a Strachan favourite, had been bought by Virginian farmers for a few pounds of tobacco. In short, Lyon and his *Colonial Advocate* made people mad: mad at him, or mad at the people who were mad at him.

He also made people choose sides. On one side was the Family Compact, rich and powerful and wanting to stay that way. On the other side were the Reformers, who thought the people should have more say in running the country. Most of the Reformers were ordinary citizens, farmers, and small merchants, but some were wealthy and respected men like Jesse Ketchum and Robert Baldwin, the doctor's son, a brave and honest man dedicated to democracy (and who later did much to bring it about).

Lyon Mackenzie's concern for the under-privileged was selective. When members of the Toronto Typographical Union—the oldest union in Canada—asked for a 10-hour day and $8 a week at the *Colonial Advocate*, Mackenzie, the defender of the poor and powerless, and tireless fighter for justice, fired them all.

**By 1826,** the VIPs in the Family Compact were seriously annoyed. After a pub crawl through York's nightspots, 15 sons of the rich and famous, with their fathers hiding smiles of approval, broke down the door of the *Colonial Advocate*. Lyon was out of town, and his young apprentices were too scared to fight

Lyon knew the Bible by heart before he was grown, and at age 11 he discovered the local library. He read everything in it and made notes on all the books, habits that continued throughout his life. He had enormous respect for the printed word, and great faith in its power to change people's hearts and minds.

back. Isobel and the children huddled upstairs while the vandals trashed everything in sight and threw the type—small blocks of metal with raised letters on one end—into the bay.

Jesse Ketchum fired off a note to Lyon and told him to come home and sue the pants off the rich kids. Lyon did.

The Black Bull, still doing business at Queen and Soho

Those smiling fathers smiled again: their friend Chief Justice William Campbell was in charge of the case, so they were sure Mackenzie would lose. They were wrong, and their smiles vanished when Judge Campbell said they had to pay Lyon £625 (about $3,000) in damages. Their sons nevertheless went on to become lawyers, judges, and politicians.

## Mayor Mackenzie

On March 6, 1834, the Town of York became the City of Toronto. Once again it bore the name bestowed centuries before: Toronto, from the Mohawk *tkaronto*, "trees standing in the water." It

With the damages awarded to him after the Type Riot, Lyon Mackenzie, who'd been just about broke, was back in business. More and more people believed what they read in his paper: too much money and too much power were held by too few. Maybe they, the ordinary people, could do something about it.

In 1828 they did: they elected Lyon to the House of Assembly. Once there, of course, he couldn't keep quiet. He was thrown out five times—and five times the people re-elected him. After that, they voted him in as the first mayor of Toronto.

His Worship Mayor William Lyon Mackenzie gave his city its coat of arms: a shield with an Aboriginal warrior leaning on one side and Britannia leaning on the other, topped by a beaver perched on a crown. Mayor Mackenzie also gave Toronto its motto: "Industry, Intelligence, Integrity." While it might not always have described the behaviour of the city's leaders, most of the time it did reflect the spirit of its people.

Both the coat of arms and the motto were replaced in 1998, following the creation of the new, giant city of Toronto. The motto is now: "Diversity Our Strength."

was a name first given to the narrow fish-filled passage (a favourite Native meeting place) between lakes Simcoe and Couchiching, which later hopscotched its way down to the shores of Lake Ontario. In a way, this renaming, this casting off of the English "York," was a sign of things to come. The little city was growing up, talking back to its parent across the ocean, testing the rules, getting ready to build a life of its own.

Apart from overseeing the birth of the City of Toronto, Mayor Lyon Mackenzie didn't do much in his few months in office. Council meetings were like gang wars; everybody argued all the

time, especially the Mayor. When the Tories beat the Reformers in the city election of 1835, Lyon went back to the House of Assembly to stir up trouble.

## Sir Francis Bonehead

Three years earlier, Mackenzie had gone to England with a list of 533 complaints about the Family Compact. But the Colonial Office in London moved about as fast as the ancient glacier; nothing had happened. Then, in 1836, Francis Bond Head, for reasons nobody has been able to figure out, was appointed lieutenant-governor of Canada. There is a story that the job was meant for his cousin Edmund and somebody got the names mixed up.

Sir Francis was handsome, adventurous, accomplished, and, in a weird coincidence, short. His feet, like Mackenzie's, didn't touch the floor when he sat in a chair. He was a soldier for years, serving under Wellington at Waterloo. Then he went to South America to mine gold and silver. While there, he earned the name "Galloping Head" for riding at top speed from Buenos Aires to the Andes and back. In a week. Twice. He mastered the lasso and pushed it as standard equipment for the cavalry, but it never caught on. So he settled down in Kent with his high-born wife and his high-born horses and his cushy job as a Poor Law

**Pioneer gate closer at Chief Justice Campbell's house, now at University and Queen**

Commissioner (something like the head of a county welfare office today). On the side, he wrote clever travel books; 32 of them are in the Toronto Reference Library. He lived until he was 82 years old, active, happy, and successful.

**Except for the** two years he spent in Toronto. As a lieutenant-governor, Bond Head bombed. He was the wrong man in the wrong place at the wrong time. Many in the city, especially the Mackenzie children, called him Bonehead, and he deserved the nickname. He did some truly stupid things, mostly because he believed, right down to his tiny polished riding boots, that he could act without the consent of the people. The Reformers were soon in a rage, especially Lyon, who threw his wig a lot during Head's rule.

Yet when Sir Francis first arrived, just before the election of 1836, people cheered. Most ordinary people were glad to see the last of his predecessor, Sir John Colborne, who had kept the Family Compact happy but made everybody else mad. The maddest of all, aside from Mackenzie, was a young Methodist minister and newspaperman named Egerton Ryerson. He had good reason: as a parting gift Colborne had handed over to Strachan and the Anglican Church 32,000 more hectares (77,000 acres) of land, just in case they ran short. The Methodists got no free land at all.

Head settled into the big two-storey, four-chimney Government House on King Street, where Roy Thomson Hall is today, to bask in the general adoration. At first he listened to the Reformers, even appointing a few to his Executive Council. But when they didn't agree with him, he stopped listening and started shouting. In a month or so all the Reformers resigned.

So Head dissolved the Assembly, called an election, and then interfered in the running of it. He said the Reformers, including pioneers like the Baldwins and Ketchums and Cawthras, were traitors. He said: "The people of Upper Canada detest democracy!" He said: "[Mackenzie] lies out of every pore in his skin. Whether he be sleeping or waking, on foot or on horseback, talking with his neighbours or writing for a newspaper, a multitudinous swarm of lies ... are buzzing and settling about him like flies around a horse in August."

Just to make sure they won the election, the Tories took out a little insurance. Only men who owned property could vote, so the Tories printed hundreds of deeds to land that didn't exist and handed them out to their supporters. And on election day they gave free booze to everybody who voted for them. It was one of the crookedest elections in Canadian history.

The Tories won. For Mackenzie, it was the last straw.

**Rebellion seemed** the only answer. Lyon went undercover, sneaking through the countryside to gather support. Farmers took down rusty muskets from their log walls and held fake turkey shoots, practising to pick off the real turkeys down in Toronto. Blacksmiths forged more pikes—walking sticks with metal spikes at the bottom—than the local barns could hold. One of these blacksmiths was Samuel Lount of Holland Landing, a big man with a big heart and a big family, who had served in the Assembly until the crooked election.

Head was told of the discontent, of Lyon's fiery speeches, of the muskets

In the middle of the night on December 4, 1837, Lieutenant-Governor Sir Francis Bond Head was rousted out of his warm bed. A rebel "army" had gathered at The Sickle and Sheath, a tavern run by John Montgomery, six kilometres (four miles) up Yonge Street near the 4th Concession (now Eglinton Avenue). The next day the streets of Toronto buzzed with fearful talk, and flocks of rumours flew about like passenger pigeons.

and the pikes. He even got an eyewitness report of farmers marching down Yonge Street. He paid no attention. He couldn't believe the rebels were serious.

## The Kids of De Grassi

Eventually, Sir Francis was persuaded to take the rebels seriously, but no one knew how big the so-called "army" was. Enter the kids of De Grassi. No, not the ones in the TV show, though the show's title does come from a street named for the De Grassis of the Rebellion. These kids were Cornelia and Charlotte, teenaged daughters of Philippe De Grassi, an Italian-born British army officer who had come to Canada in 1831 with his family.

As a war veteran, De Grassi had been granted 200 acres (81 hectares) at the forks of the Don River, near today's Taylor Creek Park. He wasn't a fan of

Cornelia De Grassi, spy and night rider, gallops down Yonge Street to safety.

Mackenzie's wild ideas, and when he heard the rumours of rebellion, he rode towards town ready to fight for Queen and Country, especially the part he owned. With him were Cornelia and Charlotte. On the way, they were stopped by rebels led by a Pickering farmer, Peter Matthews. Charlotte lied about their destination and Matthews let them go.

At Government House, De Grassi found Head in a panic. Philippe offered to check out the rebels, but Cornelia, knowing her father would likely be shot or taken prisoner, volunteered to go instead.

Off she rode, through the bitter winter afternoon, her dark cloak billowing behind her, over the frozen ruts of Yonge Street, the few lonely houses grey blurs in the dusk. She galloped past the forested land set aside for a college, past Joseph Bloor's brewery, and along the edge of Mrs. Heath's farm, Deer Park, where antlered heads lifted as she flew by, until at last she reached the wheelwright's shop next to John Montgomery's tavern, The Sickle and Sheath. She looked at a sleigh, asked the price, pretended interest—but she was secretly eyeing the confused crowd in front of Montgomery's. Most of them had no guns, she saw, and many were hardly older than she was.

She got back on her horse and turned to ride south, but the way was blocked by half a dozen men, who accused her of spying and ordered her to dismount. Just then Mackenzie, wrapped in four

Cursed as "nasty little spies" by one side, praised as heroines by the other, Cornelia and Charlotte, the kids of De Grassi, entered the pages of Toronto history.

overcoats, scrambled out of the tavern to report the capture of the Hamilton mail coach. In the excitement, Cornelia spurred her horse and got away. Musket balls sliced the air. One burrowed into her saddle, another sizzled through her skirt, before she galloped out of range.

Down Yonge Street she rode, pell-mell, the horse's breath a silver ribbon in the cold moonlight, down the steep and slippery hill below St. Clair, past the Red Lion Inn, where young couples danced a polka in the fire-lit second-floor ball-room, on and on through the frosty air, until she reached Government House. Bond Head was much relieved to hear that the rebel army was no army at all, but only a few hundred hungry men and boys carrying pikes and clubs.

Meanwhile, Charlotte, on her way back home from Toronto, rode past the dense bush where O'Connor and Broadview now intersect. The dark silence was broken by gunfire. She was wounded in one leg but still managed to make it to the farm on the River Don.

## Rout of the Rebel

The next day, big Sam Lount led about a hundred rebels down Yonge as far as College. They were ambushed by a patrol commanded by Sheriff Jarvis— who was hiding in a clump of frozen cabbages on the future site of Maple Leaf Gardens. Each side took a few shots and ran away.

On Wednesday, December 6, Sir Francis put on his favourite uniform (white), got on his favourite horse (white), and, flanked by John Strachan and John Beverley Robinson, both in black (the three of them looked like tall piano keys), trotted up Yonge Street towards Montgomery's tavern. With them were 1,000 volunteers, a fife and drum band, a sheaf of Union Jacks, and a pair of cannon.

The big guns did the trick. When Lyon led 150 men half a mile south and opened fire, a cannonball sent the rebels running north. And when Head

The Battle of Yonge Street, with top-hatted Mackenzie and speeding cannonball

Lt. Col. Robert Moodie fired the first shot of the Rebellion. Moodie was mortally wounded when a rebel fired back.

and Strachan and the rest arrived at Montgomery's tavern, they shot a cannonball through the dining-room window and all the rebels ran out. Those who weren't killed or wounded kept on running till they reached home—or the United States. The tavern was torched.

Hundreds of suspects were rounded up and sent to prison at Fort Henry, to await transportation to the penal colony in Australia. John Montgomery and Joseph Shepard were two of seven convicts who dug through the jail walls and escaped to New York. Pardoned in 1849,

they came back to Toronto. John opened another tavern on the ashes of The Sickle and Sheath. Joseph settled on a thousand acres (400 hectares) farther north, and part of that land became Sheppard Avenue, the name misspelled by a city hall clerk.

**Sam Lount and** Peter Matthews were captured, thrown in the Toronto jail, and kept in chains, with only wet blankets for warmth. (Some rebels died of pneumonia.) In the spring, John Beverley Robinson, in black again, sentenced them to hang. On April 12, 1838, despite a plea for mercy signed by 5,000 people and presented by a kneeling Mrs. Lount, despite the tears of Sheriff Jarvis, who knew both men well, Lount and Matthews were led up the 12 wooden steps to the scaffold. Samuel Lount said: "I'm not ashamed of anything I've done. I trust in God and I'll die like a man." The whole town—even the children, dressed up in party clothes—watched as he did die, instantly. Peter Matthews took a little longer, struggling hard for a minute before he was still. Twenty-three children were fatherless.

And what of William Lyon Mackenzie? After a series of narrow escapes Lyon got across the dangerous Niagara River in a rowboat to New York. Isobel and the children joined him for ten years of unhappy exile. Pardoned with the other rebels in 1849, Lyon came back to Toronto. In 1851 he was elected to the Legislature for the seventh time, where he served—quietly—until 1858.

He died on August 28, 1861, in a house at 82 Bond Street given him by friends. The house still stands.

Mackenzie's rebellion—courageous, sometimes foolhardy, marked by moments of high comedy and searing tragedy, and wonderfully captured by Toronto's Dennis Lee in the poem *1838*—changed history. In a few short years the two Canadas were one, responsible government was a fact, and democracy had begun. The Family Compact would never again rule unchallenged.

## Mud Streets, Main Streets

Charles Dickens, on vacation after writing *Nicholas Nickleby,* found Toronto a nice place to visit—except for the mud. Most tourists agreed with him. A popular joke—outside Toronto—went like this: "A man walking along King Street sees a hat on the road. He picks it up, and sees the head of its owner, deep in mud. Horrified, the man says to the head: 'Hold on! We'll soon get you out of there!' The head says: 'Never mind me! It's the horse I'm riding that's really in trouble!'"

## 1838 to 1867

## Bright Lights, Big City

The yellow building in the foreground, known as the Coffin Block because of its shape, houses the stagecoach office of William Weller—the place where all journeys by road begin and end. Passengers often have to get out and push the stage when it gets stuck in the mud, which is everywhere. One of Toronto's first street lights was put on this very important corner. The red wagon nearby, soon to see action in the Great Fire of 1849, is a pumper called the British America. The third floor of the Coffin Block is an annex for the overflow of guests from the Wellington Hotel, which around this time changed its name from the Ontario House. John Grantham, who runs the livery stable near disreputable Henrietta Lane, also owns a billy goat that terrorizes any child who wanders too near. Behind the stable, in "The Big Field," are the winter quarters of George Bernard's travelling circus.

**The** roads were a mess. Earlier, homeowners and businessmen had managed to pry enough money out of the Assembly to "macadamize" Dundas, Kingston, and Yonge. A macadamized road, named after Scottish landowner John McAdam, who invented it, is made with layers of broken and crushed stone, packed down hard. It's built slightly above the surrounding area so water will drain off it.

Now these same property owners went after more money, and dollar by dollar, block by block, some downtown thoroughfares were improved. Where they couldn't afford gravel, they planked: many streets were laid with long flat boards, which slowly warped and rotted and turned to mush. Wooden sidewalks—boardwalks, like those in the Beach area today—made it a little easier to get around, although they turned out to be a bad idea, as we shall see.

**By the middle** of the century, with the population pushing 30,000, Toronto had a water system too—of a sort. From 1834 on, in fits and starts and dribbles, whenever the council got a few dollars together, a few miles of pipe were laid through the downtown area. The pipe and the few hydrants connected to it—far too few to satisfy the volunteer fire department or the dozens of dogs run-

ning loose—were mostly for factories and big business. People still used their own backyard wells—usually too near their own backyard privies—or one of the half-dozen public pumps around town. And many bought water from a cart, the way you might buy a bag of popcorn or a basket of apples today. It wasn't until the 1880s that most Toronto homes had tap water.

In any event, after the sun went down, you couldn't see the mud, or the roads, or the sidewalks, or the hydrants, or even the dogs—until the glorious night of December 28, 1841, when everybody trooped downtown to view the newfangled invention: street lights. They were gas lamps, set on fancy black

Nobody drank much water in Victorian Toronto; alcohol was by far the beverage of choice. Everyone drank it, even the children. Teachers drank before they taught a class, preachers before they gave a sermon, lawyers and judges in the courtroom, and politicians most of the time. At mid-century, Toronto had 152 taverns and 206 beer shops, and if they ran out, you could always buy the stuff at your local grocery store. Beer cost 15 cents a gallon, rum 2 cents a glass. More than half the people in jail were there because they were drunk. How the city got the nickname "Toronto the Good" is utterly baffling.

**The mystery of the disappearing rider,
or the hatless horseman**

iron poles, and there were a hundred of them along King Street. Each lamp gave as much light as 10 candles, and the gas, made from coal, was sold by a company that eventually became Consumers' Gas and then Enbridge Consumers' Gas, which now cooks the food and warms the bodies of half the people in the city. The founder of Consumers' Gas was Charles Berczy, the first postmaster of Toronto and the son of Little Albert. Children followed the lamplighter on his evening rounds, watching in wonder as he pushed his long torch under the six-sided glass shades to ignite the wicks. You can read all about it in Bernice Thurman Hunter's book *Lamplighter*.

**Each night,** the stores and structures along the main drag glowed with fuzzy light: Beckett's Apothecary Shop, with its big brass-bound windows; Klingenbrumer's Clock Repair; Campbell & Hunter Saddlers; Nordheimer's Music Store; St. James' Cathedral, the fourth one, built after a fire in 1839; Harris' Hardware Store, said to be fireproof; the red-brick bulk of the *Patriot* newspaper; a hatter's, a tailor's, a clothier's, an ice cream parlour, the many hotels, and the many, many taverns.

But the most dramatic light of all was seen in the early morning of Saturday, April 7, 1849. And it nearly destroyed the town.

## The First Great Fire

It was an hour past midnight. Sensible folk were sound asleep. The night watchman was on the job. The town was peaceful, free of danger. Or so he thought.

Nobody saw that first curl of smoke, that first finger of flame, in the shadows of the stable behind Covey's Inn, just east of Jarvis on the north side of King Street. It may have started when a stable-boy tripped over a lantern, or when the hot ash from a careless customer's cigar dropped on the dry straw. It may have started when a business rival set a match to it: in the 1800s, half the fires in Toronto were started on purpose.

Nobody knows. But once the fire started, there was little to stop it.

**It spread** from the straw to the pine board floors, to the stalls, to the walls, to the wood-shingled roof, to the shed next door, to the rickety stable beyond. It was only then that the alarm—the big bell of St. James' Cathedral, soon to melt—rang out. The flames raced north, south, east, west. Three hours later, most of downtown Toronto was ablaze, and the fire was no longer a fire. It was a *conflagration*, a word that means "a burning together," used by an insurance company when a fire destroys more than a million dollars' worth of property.

A half-mile (0.8 km) from the fire, Egerton Ryerson found embers in his backyard, and John Strachan, who didn't even wake up until his church had burned down, later reported that scorched

**Let there be light!**

During the Great Fire of 1849, 6 hectares (15 acres) of flames, from George Street to Church, from Adelaide to King, leaped up into the night, and were seen as far away as St. Catharines. The heat reached 1100°C, the same temperature as lava. It was hot enough to melt gold and silver and copper and lead. It was hot enough to melt tin—which was what the roofs on the brick houses were made of. It was hot enough to vapourize rat poison and blood and to make its own winds, great surges of air that hurled burning wood and cinders and ash high into the sky, and dropped them blocks away to start other fires.

wood was carried two miles (3.2 km). Soot lay thick on the tents of George Bernard's Circus, across from the Coffin Block on Wellington.

As fires go, it was a beaut. And those wooden sidewalks were a big help. The wood was extra fuel, for one thing; for another, the sidewalks were built above-ground, so air could rush in underneath them to help the fire along. Some older houses and shops, and all of the sheds and stables—full of hay and straw—were wooden, with wooden shingles on the roofs. And many of the buildings were taverns or dry goods shops or hardware stores. The taverns were full of liquor. The dry goods shops were full of cloth. The hardware stores—including the fireproof

Harris store, which burned nicely—were full of paint and oil. Wood, hay, straw, liquor, cloth, paint, oil: a perfect recipe for a fabulous fire. In the path of the fire were two newspaper offices, the *Patriot* and the *Mirror*, their wooden shelves piled high with sheets of newsprint, excellent fuel. Both were reduced to ashy ruin. And in the rubble of the *Patriot* lay the charred body of the Great Fire's only victim, Richard Watson, overcome by smoke while helping to salvage supplies.

**The firemen** worked hard, but the puny trickles from the tanks atop their horse-drawn wagons did little; the water carters raced hither and yon—whoever got to a fire first won five dollars, which may explain the arson count—but they raced so recklessly that most of the water spilled into the rutted street; the soldiers

**The first Toronto streetcar**

from the Fort helped where they could— but helped themselves to a few barrels of beer, too. The hydrants were few and far between, and mostly in the wrong part of town; and the Water Company burned down, which caused a snicker or two. In short, it was a disaster. The core of Toronto was a blackened waste.

But the spirit of the young city was sure and steady. Within days the cleanup began, and the next ten years saw a big building boom, made even bigger when the railways came to town.

## Making Tracks

In the 1850s, as the population climbed past 40,000, the wealthy members of the old Family Compact, who still owned all those magnificent 200-acre (81 hectare) park lots north of Queen, saw a chance to make a bundle. They subdivided. Soon, homes and shops and small factories and businesses dotted the landscape all the way up to Bloor, east to the Don, and

At the time of the Great Fire, there were horse-drawn ten-seater carriages that took people up Yonge Street to Yorkville, but such travel soon wore out the horses, the carriages, the drivers, and, not least, the customers. Think about it: potholes, ruts, rotting planks that sank every now and then, no tires on the wheels, and the shock absorber 50 years in the future. There was too much shake and rattle, and very little roll.

Lady Elgin, steaming

King and Queen had tracks too. "The Better Way" had arrived.

## Making More Tracks

west to Dufferin Street. No longer was it possible to walk around Toronto in an hour. It was time for mass transit.

Somebody got the bright idea of making tracks for wheels to ride smoothly on, and in 1861 a set of rails was laid down on Yonge from the St. Lawrence Market to the Red Lion Inn above Bloor. These horsecars ran every half-hour, 16 hours a day in summer, 14 hours a day in winter, when, open to the weather and without a stove, the passengers nearly froze to death. The speed limit was six miles (10 km) an hour, and the fare was a nickel. Very soon,

Lady Elgin, the white-gloved, well-hatted, wasp-waisted wife of the Governor General, turned over a spadeful of earth on October 15, 1851, and Toronto's first railway, the Ontario, Simcoe & Huron, was born. As a reward, the first engine was named after her. It cost $9,000, it burned wood, and its top was bigger than its bottom. The line ran 19 kilometres (12 miles) north, along the old trail of the Toronto Carrying Place that Brûlé had walked 235 years before. By 1858, the line had become the Northern Railway and ran all the way to

The dream of architect John Howard—to turn the lakeside into a beautiful park where children could swim and play, where their parents could promenade in the healthful air—was turned into a nightmare by railroad tracks. The city council caved in to pressure from the railway owners. They were, so to speak, railroaded. The docklands are still being fixed up after decades of neglect.

Collingwood. Ten years later it had company: The Great Western, which ran from Toronto to Sarnia, Windsor, and New York; and the Grand Trunk, which stretched from Toronto east to Montreal and Quebec, and west to Guelph, London, and Goderich. Nineteen kilometres of track had become over 3,000. And all of these railroad lines came together on Toronto's waterfront.

Although the huge railway development didn't do much for the scenery, it was a big spur to industry. New factories to serve the railroads, and businesses to serve the factories, sprang up everywhere. Toronto bubbled with energy and wallowed in money. Banks burst forth overnight on every corner, like mushrooms in the dark: the Bank of Nova Scotia, the Bank of Commerce, the Bank of British North America, the Bank of Toronto, the Bank of Montreal, the Ontario Bank—this last built by Joseph Sheard, who thirty years before had refused to build the scaffold that hanged Sam Lount. And all of them spawned branches out in the suburbs of Brockton and Parkdale and Seaton Village and Yorkville and Riverside (which we call Riverdale). A stock exchange appeared on Wellington Street, to make the money travel faster and farther.

Toronto had hit the big time, and the railroad had brought it there. The railroad ushered in the blessings of the Industrial Revolution, and also its curse. It altered Toronto deeply; it linked Toronto with everywhere else. It wove Canada together.

## The Lamp of Learning

It wasn't just the street lamps that were lit. By 1850 the lamp of learning—the symbol of the Toronto Board of

The Enoch Turner schoolhouse, Toronto's first free school (for Protestant Irish kids), now a favourite place for weddings and banquets, but no longer free

In 1849, Robert Baldwin's Reform government decided they must reduce Anglican land and property holdings, so they took King's College from Bishop Strachan, cut its ties to the church, and turned it into the University of Toronto. Strachan ranted about the "godless university" for a couple of years, then set up Trinity College, which is still a very Anglican place, and haunted by its founder. Trinity students swear they see John Strachan's ghost every November 1, the day he died in 1867.

Education—began to glow in earnest. And it's at this point that A. (for Adolphus) Egerton Ryerson comes into our story again.

Egerton was born in 1803 near Long Point, on Lake Erie, to parents who were well off, Anglican, and Loyalist. His uncle Samuel Ryerse (a spelling mistake by an army clerk, which still lives in Port Ryerse on the map of Ontario) had served with Simcoe during the American Revolution, and got 3,400 hectares (8,400 acres) of prime land as a reward.

Young Egerton broke with the family religion and by 24 was a Methodist minister. His sermons were real barnburners, and it was always standing-room-only at the church. He was something to look at, too, with a strong jaw, a nose that could saw timber, deep eyes afire with intelligence and passion, and a firm, full mouth. He fought with John Strachan about all the land given to the Anglicans—and he won. The Methodists (and the Baptists, and the Lutherans, and the Catholics) were given some free land too. On some of it, in Cobourg, Egerton built Victoria College, which moved to Queen's Park Circle in 1891.

For a time Egerton had supported Lyon Mackenzie, but he balked at guns. His weapons were the pulpit, the press—he founded what is now the *United Church Observer*, and the Ryerson half of the McGraw-Hill Ryerson publishing company—and the public school.

Popular nineteenth-century pub, Tecumseh's Wigwam, really a log cabin, at Bloor Street and Avenue Road

**It is Egerton Ryerson** you can thank—or blame—for the fact that you go to school. Not only did he say that all children, rich, poor, and in between, had the *right* to go to school without paying for it, but he also said that they *must* go to school. Ontario's free public schools— a system soon copied by other provinces— were his idea. They aren't quite free, of course: they're paid for by the government, with tax money collected from citizens.

What Egerton didn't say but secretly thought was that school would keep the poor kids from running wild. Canada was changing from a rural to an urban society, and children who once worked all day on the farm were now hanging out downtown. The upper class, including Egerton, actually believed, strange as it sounds to us, that poor and working-class children tended to be criminal and

The 1857 printing of the threepenny beaver stamp of 1851, worth about $4,000.

destructive *by nature*: they were born that way. So, if all the poor kids were imprisoned in school, and brainwashed to respect property and obey orders, then the rich folks could rest easy, and keep what they already had most of: money and power. It was a neat solution.

Trained teachers were Egerton's idea too. (In fact, he ran the whole show for 40 years.) In 1852 he set up, where Ryerson University is now, what he called Toronto Normal School, to turn out "normal" teachers. Normal teachers were those who used the same methods in every school in the province. Before then, a teacher didn't need any special training.

About the same time as Egerton was pushing the Three Rs, Enoch Turner gave away a lot of the money he'd made from selling beer to build the first free school in Toronto. (This was partly because the

The older city schools were dour places, where there was little mixing of boys and girls. You can still see, etched in stone above separate doors at these schools, BOYS and GIRLS. There was no gym. No lockers. No pool. No resource centre. No nurse. No washrooms. No guidance counsellor. But there was lots of memory work: multiplication tables, kings and queens, battles, countries, mountains, rivers, hundreds of poems, hundreds of songs.

city ran out of money for a year or so, and the other schools had to close.) The Enoch Turner Schoolhouse on King Street opened its thick wooden doors in 1848. And it's still open. You can visit it to find out what school was like all those years ago: slates instead of paper or a computer screen; a slate pencil rather than a ballpoint; benches instead of your own desk and chair; a switch or a leather strap in place of detentions; jacks and spinning-tops on the board sidewalk for the little kids and, across the street behind some shrubs, boxing and cock-fighting for the bigger kids.

One of the songs every schoolchild learned was "The Maple Leaf Forever," composed in 1867—when Canada became a country and Toronto became the capital of the province of Ontario— by schoolteacher Alexander Muir. One autumn day Mr. Muir and Mr. Leslie (who owned a plant nursery at Pape and Queen, and had a street named after him) went for a walk. They were talking about a Patriotic Song Contest when a maple leaf fell on Mr. Leslie's coat sleeve. He had trouble brushing it off. Mr. Muir laughed and said, "The maple leaf forever." The rest is history. He wrote the words and music in two hours, won second prize in the contest, printed 1,000 copies of it, and taught it to his students. A music company stole it and made a pile of money. Every schoolchild in Toronto sang it for the next 80 years. The first verse goes like this:

*In days of yore, from Britain's shore*
*Wolfe, the dauntless hero, came,*
*And planted firm Britannia's flag*
*On Canada's fair domain.*
*Here may it wave, our boast, our pride,*
*And joined in love together,*
*The Thistle, Shamrock, Rose entwine*
*The Maple Leaf forever!*

We don't sing it any more: it's hopelessly British, and it has nothing to do with the Toronto of today, with its many cultures and races. But it made its author

St. Lawrence Hall, named for Canada's patron saint, was built in 1850.

In 1880, when *Globe* founder George Brown had just settled down to a happy home life with his wife, Anne, and their three children, he was shot in the leg by a fired employee, also named George, whom he'd never seen before, and who had meant to kill the head printer. The wound got infected, and after 45 days of pain and fever, George Brown died. The other George was hanged.

famous for a time. When he died suddenly in 1906, all the children in Gladstone School, where he was principal, showed up wearing maple leaves. Gladstone School is now Alexander Muir–Gladstone. And if you go to 62 Laing Street, near the corner of Queen and Leslie, you can still see the tree from which that maple leaf fell.

## Diversions and Excursions

Reading and writing weren't just what you did in school. You could choose any one of eight newspapers, more than the city boasts now. The best was run by George Brown, a young Scotsman who founded the *Globe* in 1844. At first a weekly, it soon had many readers, especially after it serialized a brand-new novel by Charles Dickens, *Dombey and Son*. By 1853 it was a daily. Brown got into politics, hobnobbed with Sir John A.

Macdonald, and became a Father of Confederation: it was largely because of his skill at making deals that Canada as a nation was born. His *Globe* newspaper eventually merged with the *Mail and Empire,* in 1936, and is now known as the *Globe and Mail*, "Canada's national newspaper."

When your nose wasn't stuck in a newspaper, you could watch the play *Rip Van Winkle* in the two-storey brick Royal Lyceum Theatre at King and Bay. Just across the park from St. James Cathedral, in the 1,000-seat auditorium of the new St. Lawrence Hall, you could listen one night to the silver tongues of Sir John A. Macdonald and George Brown, and the next to the golden soprano of Jenny Lind, the "Swedish Nightingale," whose range was from B below middle C to high G. Three notes higher and she could have cracked glass.

**Horse-powered ferry to Toronto Island**

You could play a piano bought from the German carpenter Theodore Heintzman, who made them in his kitchen at 288 Annette Street.

After April 1858, when a storm washed away part of the peninsula, you could ride a ferry to what was now the Island, where you could have a picnic, take a hike, or just hang out. Eight months later, when the thermometer hit a record –33°C on January 10 and the lake froze solid, you could *walk* to the Island.

You could go to P.T. Barnum's Grand Colossal Museum and Menagerie on the "Fair Green," beside the jail, and there you'd see:

A Team of Ten Elephants
Six Beautiful Lions
A Sacred Burmese Bull
A Monster White or Polar Bear
A Magnificent Royal Tigress—
the LARGEST ever captured ALIVE!
An Infantile Camel
A Native Ceylon Chief
The AMAZING Mr. Nellis, the Man without Arms, who will load and fire a pistol with his TOES; cut Profile likenesses, shoot at a target with a Bow and Arrow; play the Accordion AND the Cello
AND ...
THE REAL, GENUINE, ORIGINAL!!
GENERAL TOM THUMB, 20 YEARS OLD, 15 POUNDS IN WEIGHT, TWENTY-EIGHT INCHES HIGH, WHO WILL GIVE HIS FAMOUS IMPERSONATIONS OF NAPOLEON AND FREDERICK THE GREAT.

All for a mere 25 CENTS, a Quarter of a Dollar, a BARGAIN!

Nowadays, putting human beings in a zoo, and paying to see them, is horrifying to us (as well as illegal), but a hundred years ago nobody raised an eyebrow. Twenty million people, including Queen Victoria, saw Tom Thumb (Charles Stratton), and Barnum, a master of hype, the "Prince of Humbugs," got very rich.

As Canada celebrated its birth, Toronto—prosperous, busy, hopeful, growing bigger every day—felt it deserved its title of The Queen City of the West.

**Pioneer woman and curious companion**

### Mean Streets

There were places in the Queen City where no lamp glowed, no light fell. If Toronto had its main streets, glowing and rich, it also had its mean streets, shadowed, grimy, and shockingly poor. Many immigrants, pouring in from the country, from a starving Ireland, a crowded Scotland, from a Europe torn by revolt or war, found jobs that paid little, or no jobs at all. They lived in shacks near the Don, on Elizabeth and Lombard streets, on lower Bathurst and on south Jarvis, where the railway tracks ran along the waterfront.

1868 to 1904

**Brighter
Lights,
Bigger City**

The big changes here are the telegraph wires, linking Toronto to the rest of the world, and the tracks for the horse-drawn street-cars. The wooden Wellington Hotel is gone; in its place is the stone Bank of Toronto. With the Stock Exchange to the west, this area is now the financial hub of the city. The "Big Field" remains a favourite playground for children. To its left is the only building in this picture that still stands, just north of Berczy Park on Wellington; when you go down-town, look for Vines Wine Bar and Bistro. On Front Street— now farther back from the lake because of landfill—two mem-bers of the Dauntless Baseball Club talk over the batting order.

**A** neighbourhood near George and Adelaide streets was called Fish Alley and described like this:

*This lane contains nine apologies for houses and is inhabited by fifty souls. There are no backyards to these miserable hovels, and slops, filth, and dirt are thrown out in front of the doors. At one end of the lane the necessary [an outside toilet] is in fearful state, and ... a well, situated a short distance from it, receives the sewage ...*

Another writer said of a place on Jarvis Street near the lake:

*You enter a house from the front door and find yourself in a room 12 by 14 feet, in which are huddled together, as if they are frightened to look at their fellow-creatures, a man, five women, three boys, and two [babies] in arms. The stove is almost reddened with heat ... the walls are so black one would think [it] was their original colour, and ... The stench of the pig-pen within three feet of the back door is so foul you could cut it with a knife.*

A few doors further down was "a house the rear room of which is occupied by a

Children at work delivering coal

Some children from the mean streets worked—for pennies a day—in the new mills and factories, or sewing shirts and overcoats at home, or selling newspapers, or shining shoes, or cleaning houses for rich people, or looking after their little sisters and brothers while their parents worked. Some of them begged. Some of them shoplifted. There were now more shops to lift from.

brigade of pigs." An open door led to a room where people cooked, ate, and slept.

The children of these houses didn't go to school very often or very long, even though the truant officer or the cops were out to get them. Street kids—then as now—were hassled. A boy of nine was shot dead by a policeman when he didn't get off somebody's dock fast enough. For playing ball in the street, three boys were fined two dollars. They couldn't pay it, so they were sent to jail—the new jail on the banks of the Don, or perhaps the Central Prison south of King Street on Strachan, where beatings, solitary confinement, and terror were the rule. In the next cell there might have been a member of the Brooks Bush gang, a bunch of thugs who lived in the ravine near Castle Frank and regularly robbed, mugged, or murdered their fellow citizens.

**The first Eaton's, at the corner of Queen and Yonge streets**

## "T. Eaton & Co., Drygoods"

On the morning of December 8, 1869, a young Irishman named Timothy Eaton opened a dry goods store on the corner of Queen and Yonge. It was about the size of a two-car garage, and helping Timothy out were two men clerks, who earned six dollars a week; one woman clerk, who earned two dollars less than the men; a boy who ran errands, swept floors, and did all the grunt work for a dollar a week; and Maggie the Wonder Horse, who pulled the delivery wagon for a bag of oats and a sugar cube.

Timothy's shopping rules were unheard of: all sales cash, no credit, no haggling—the price on the item is what you pay—and a money-back guarantee. And then he held the first sidewalk sale in history, putting big bins of five-cent ties and one-cent spools of thread in front of the store.

People laughed. They said he wasn't playing with a full deck.

In a way, this was true: for a long time he wouldn't sell playing cards. He thought they were sinful. He wouldn't sell tobacco either.

They came to laugh—but they stayed to shop. The little store grew and grew and grew. Eaton's was the first store in Canada with an escalator, an elevator, and a mail-order catalogue. (But not the first with a telephone: druggist Joseph Lee put a phone in both of his east end stores in 1877, a year after Bell invented it.)

Timothy Eaton's friend Robert Simpson opened a store right across the street in 1872. Between them they put a hammerlock on shopping, and the centre of Toronto, the focus, the place to be, shifted westward to Queen and Yonge.

For a hundred years Eaton's catalogue was in more Canadian homes than the Bible. It helped to homogenize the nation: country folk and city folk, from sea to sea, could own identical pyjamas and dolls and ice skates and laxatives and wallpaper. You could buy everything from the catalogue: hair dye and hog fences, bunion pads and buggy wheels, freckle cream and furnaces (and the coal to burn in them). You could buy a windmill. You could buy a car. And you could certainly buy a bible.

## Phantoms of the Opera

Given Timothy's views on sin, he was definitely not at the Grand Opera House, two blocks south on Adelaide Street, on the rainy Saturday afternoon of March 19, 1881. On that day superstar Sarah Bernhardt, a.k.a. "The Divine," a.k.a. "The Golden Voice," played the lead in *Camille*. Written by Alexandre (*The Three Musketeers*) Dumas, *Camille* was an X-rated sizzler. So was Sarah. At 36, she'd gone through a list of lovers as long as her silk-stockinged leg. Preachers called her evil; Catholics were forbidden to see her; mothers locked up their daughters when she was in town; and in Kansas and Iowa and Michigan, people threw stones at her. She ducked the stones, laughed at the preachers, and went on being the most successful actress in the world. Her Toronto performance was as magnificent as its setting.

The Grand Opera House lived up to its name. Three storeys high, with a massive pillared entrance and a tower, it seated 1,600 people, with room for 500 to stand. It had a sunken orchestra pit, a huge stage that covered two-thirds of the floor, and a lighting system that was the envy of all other theatres: an automatic electric spark could light all the gas jets at once. The balconies led to fire escapes, and the stage boasted two hydrants. On the night of November 28, 1879, however, after a performance of Shakespeare's tragedy *Macbeth*, they didn't help a bit.

Not only does *Macbeth* have more murders and blood and general scariness than *Nightmare on Elm Street*, but it also *attracts* disaster. Throughout its four centuries on the stage, it's been plagued by spooky accidents. Many actors think

Davenport railway station was built in 1857, just above Davenport Road on Caledonia Park Road.

it has a curse on it and they won't say its name aloud. That wintry night in Toronto only added to the legend.

Everybody thought the fire under the three witches' big kettle was out. The audience was long gone, the janitor had locked the big front door, the actors were busy celebrating at the Queen's Hotel on Front. At midnight the black embers of the witches' fire suddenly glowed pink, then red, and burst into flame. By three o'clock the building was ablaze: the heavy velvet curtains, the carved armchairs of the private boxes, the chandeliers, the carpets, the sheet music and the wooden music stands, the 1,600 seats. The fire department, now 36 full-time, paid men, managed to save the outside, but inside, amid the charred wreckage, they found the bodies of theatre carpenter Robert Wright, his wife, and their 10-year-old daughter. One tragedy had brought about another.

Owner Alexander Manning, who later had a street named after him, rebuilt the place in 51 days flat, and next to the New York Metropolitan, it was the best opera house in North America.

**The Grand** eventually became less grand. First it was turned into a vaudeville theatre, big on jugglers and pie-in-the-face comedy routines, and then a silent movie house, where in 1924 it hosted the world premiere of *Dorothy Vernon of Haddon Hall*, starring Toronto-born Mary Pickford. In 1928 it was torn down. Toronto hasn't had a proper opera house since.

In 1919, Ambrose Small, a secretive and stingy fellow who had bought the Opera House in 1903, simply disappeared. One morning he sold a theatre chain, deposited a million and a half in the bank, had lunch with his wife, dropped into the Opera House, dropped out of the Opera House—and dropped off the face of the earth. Despite a hunt that went on for years and two rewards offered by his wife ($50,000 alive, $15,000 dead), Ambrose Small—dead or alive—never showed up.

## Animal Stories

Two blocks away and three years later, in 1882, another kind of tragedy unfolded at Harry Piper's Front Street Zoo. Harry, who already owned an elephant, a beaver, some ducks, a huge turtle named Tom, and the carcass of a 16-metre (53-foot) sperm whale (until it went bad), was given an alligator by a Florida fan. It was the first alligator ever seen in Canada, but it wasn't seen for long: it tried to swallow Tom the Turtle and choked to death.

Animals, alive and dead and sometimes in between, were much in the news in this period. Jumbo was one of them. Captured as a baby, this African elephant grew to be 3.7 metres (12 feet) high and 6,000 kilograms (13,000 pounds), the biggest elephant in captivity. He came to town in 1883, on tour with P.T. Barnum's Circus. Two years later, at age 24—young for an elephant—he was struck by a train and killed near St. Thomas.

Hogs—always a highlight of Toronto's history—hit the headlines too. Butcher William Davies, who had come to Toronto in the boom years of the 1850s and had a chain of stores all over Ontario, streamlined his slaughterhouse at the mouth of the Don. In 1874 he set up the first production line in Canada for killing pigs. His company would later become part of Canada Packers. The animal world got

John Ross Robertson, the founder of the *Evening Telegram*, gave much to the city he loved. He poured millions into Sick Kids Hospital, and each Christmas Eve, he dressed up as Santa Claus and brought gifts to every child in the hospital. He built a home on the Island for children who needed long-term care. He put up the money for a milk pasteurization plant. He gave hundreds of valuable Canadian books to the Toronto Public Library. A school on Glengrove Avenue is named after him.

its revenge on William: he died some years later after being butted by a goat.

These events, and citizen anger over the heavy loads and beatings suffered by the horses that pulled the streetcars, led to the founding of the Toronto Humane Society in 1887, to stop cruelty to animals.

## Sick Kids

As a kind of afterthought, the Humane Society also tried to help abused children. Many of them were bandaged and nursed in a narrow, three-storey, 11-room house at 31 Avenue Street, right in the middle of the slums between University Avenue and Elizabeth Street. This house was the first Hospital for Sick Children, founded by Elizabeth McMaster and several women friends in 1875. For most of a decade the energetic and devoted Elizabeth ran the hospital, coaxing money and equipment out of Toronto's rich businessmen—and looking after four children and a sick husband on the side. When her husband, Sam, died in 1888, she went to Chicago and trained as a nurse, returning to her beloved hospital in 1890 as superintendent. Elizabeth died in 1903 when she was only 56 years old, but her spirit lives on in what some think is the best children's hospital in the world.

One of the rich businessmen approached by Elizabeth was John Ross Robertson, who took a special interest in the hospital after his only daughter, Goldie, died of scarlet fever. Born in 1841, John loved the news game. He started a school newspaper while at Upper Canada College, and after graduation published the *Grumbler*, a weekly that poked fun at everybody. Following a stint at the *Globe*—during which he went west to interview Louis Riel in the midst of the Red River Rebellion, a caper that landed him in jail for a week—he founded the *Evening Telegram* in 1876. It was four pages long, and it sold for two cents. A big booster of the Empire, the Tories, and the Protestant church, the *Tely* flourished for 95 years.

**World champ rower Ned Hanlan**

John Ross Robertson became so involved in the Hospital for Sick Children that he muscled in and took over, saying he wanted to "remove the burden ... from weak women"— although there were no weak women in sight. He finally forced Elizabeth McMaster and her friends to resign from the hospital board. Some of these women then founded the Home for Incurable Children, now the Bloorview MacMillan Centre.

## Strokes and Spokes ...

After the big blow of 1858, the Islands got more popular than ever. A fisherman named John Hanlan, who cleverly saw he could catch more suckers than trout, built a big hotel on the western point, where the Simcoes' ship had anchored many years before. It was soon joined by an amusement park; fancy summer homes for the rich; cottages to rent; bicycle trails; a string of taverns (until they got so rowdy the cops closed them down); grocery stores; two bathhouses (for women only: it wasn't considered "proper" for "ladies" to swim in public, one of the thousand stupidities that cramped women's lives); and the famous Diving Horse of Hanlan's Point, who wowed the paying customers by leaping into the lake from a platform 7.6 metres (25 feet) high. A church was built too, and according to a reporter for the *Empire*, none too soon. He wrote: "... shopgirls go to the island and there they fall into the hands of some human hound who is looking for [an] innocent girl to entrap." There is also, incredible as it may seem, an account of a wild party on the Island during a teachers' convention. John's son Ned had to row back and forth across the lake to go to school every day. All this exercise later paid off. Handsome, curly-haired Ned Hanlan became the Gretzky of rowing. Crowned the world champ in 1880, he won more than 300 races in his lifetime, and was Canada's first world-famous athlete.

In winter you could skate on the bay or on Grenadier Pond—where those soldiers drowned in 1813—or ski and snowshoe and toboggan in High Park. The rest of the year you could ride your bicycle.

Towards the end of the nineteenth century, Toronto went bike-mad. Even

Leaping horse at Hanlan's Point

though they cost the enormous sum of $100—which back then would pay for 2,000 loaves of bread, 3,200 streetcar tickets, and six months' rent on an eight-room house—just about everybody bought a bike. The city had 90 stores selling nothing but bicycles. In 1895, a traffic cop reported that nearly 400 cyclists passed the corner of Yonge and King between 6 and 6:30 p.m. every day. By the following year, 200,000 Canadians had bikes.

**Women go wild
about wheels**

Some older people, afraid that bicycling gave
kids too much freedom, called it a "vulgar,
indecent craze," which would "lead girls into
reckless ways." These were the same people
who wanted to ban posters of ballet dancers
and forbid the reading of novels on Sundays.

### ... and Strikes

But even bicycling (and cricket and
lacrosse) took a back seat to a new sport
played with nine men on a diamond-
shaped field. Base ball—it was two
words at first—had come to Toronto.
Long played by kids and college students for fun, in the 1870s it began to be
played for money. The first semi-pro
team in Toronto was the Dauntless, who
played at the old "ball yard" at Broadview
and Queen, and once lost to the Boston
Red Stockings by a score of 68–0. It cost
a dime to get in. The Clippers—paid
$4,231.42 per season—played in Queen's
Park and the Toronto Maple Leafs in a
stadium at Hanlan's Point. There, on
September 5, 1914, a 19-year-old pitcher
for the Providence Grays hit his first
home run, right into Toronto Bay. His
name was Babe Ruth, and his team won
9–0. The Leafs later played in Maple
Leaf Stadium at the foot of Bathurst
Street. And now, after a dozen years in
old Exhibition Stadium, the Blue Jays
call the SkyDome home.

**Strikes of** a different sort were popular too. By the early 1870s the printers,
the carpenters, the shoemakers, the
bricklayers, and many other workers had
formed unions. They wanted more
money and shorter hours. The printers at
the *Globe* went on strike, and George
Brown got so mad he dragged them all
into court and charged them with trea-
son. The moulders at Hart Massey's factory over by the prison went on strike,
and hard-nosed Hart (who gave us
Massey Hall and Hart House, and whose
descendants included a movie star and a
governor general) got so mad he locked
them out and wouldn't let them back in
till they swore they'd never join a union.

Such arrogance later led writer B.K. Sandwell to note:

*Toronto has no social classes—*
*Only the Masseys and the masses.*

The railway workers went out on strike too, without much luck. Workers and unions finally got some respect ten years later: they marched in Canada's first Labour Day Parade, in 1886 at the Canadian National Exhibition.

## The "Ex"

Ever since 1820, in all the little towns of Upper Canada, there had been little fall fairs to show off turnips and pumpkins and bulls. Then, in 1846, all the little towns got together to put on one big fall fair for the whole province. At first this provincial fair was movable: in Brantford one year, Cobourg the next, London the year after. Toronto's movers and shakers figured it would be smarter to have it every year in the same spot—in Toronto. That way, thousands of people would spend thousands of dollars—in Toronto. The hotels and shops and restaurants and theatres and saloons would make a lot of money. And so would the movers and shakers.

They started with the Palace of Industry. Built in 1858 on King Street, just south of the Lunatic Asylum, and completely covered in glass, it was soon dubbed the Crystal Palace. It was one storey high, 78 metres (256 feet) long, and 29 metres (96 feet) wide—smaller than a football field but bigger than a hockey rink. Under all that glass were the very latest products and inventions, including wax fruit, machine-made lace collars, and horse blankets. The Palace was designed by Sandford Fleming, who had a hand in building half the railroads and bridges in the country. He also designed the first Canadian postage stamp (see page 59), and found time to invent time: it was Sandford Fleming who devised the Standard Time Zones the whole world now uses.

**The Crystal Palace was constructed in 1858 as a copy of the London, England, original. It was moved to the Exhibition Grounds, where it burned down in 1906.**

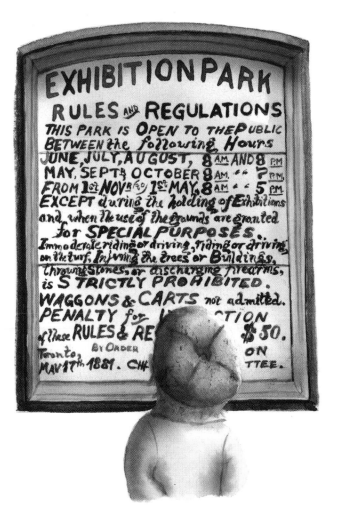

The Ex rules! An 1881 sign at the entrance to Exhibition Park, forbidding, among other things, "the discharge of firearms."

**In 1878,** the city council rented some land from the army near Dufferin Street, and the Crystal Palace was moved, pane by pane, strut by strut, to the spot where the French had traded rum for furs 120 years earlier at Fort Rouillé. Another storey was tucked in underneath—which seems a risky way to do it—and a pointy tower was added. Twenty-two buildings sprang up around it; one week of exhibits grew to two; and what had been known as the Toronto Industrial Exhibition became the Canadian National Exhibition (CNE).

It was the biggest show on earth. It still is. In its first year 100,000 people paid a quarter each to get in. The ticket price was the same for the next 60 years.

There were 8,234 things to see: a bagpipe contest, a dog and cat show, a better rat trap, the best pies and pickles and jams and quilts in Ontario, as the pioneer women showed off their stuff, the fattest pig/cheese/cabbage/petunia in the known universe, and races of all kinds—foot, horse, boat, balloon, and bicycle.

Later, in the sideshows—which were just that, shows off to one side, not as important as the main exhibits—you could gawk at Jo-Jo the Dog-Faced Boy, Stella, half man and half woman, the Alligator Man from the Florida Swamp, and, if you could stand it, the Wild Man of Borneo as he tore apart a chicken and ate it before your very eyes. All of these so-called "freaks" were really fakes— but people flocked to see them anyway.

There was even a ride. It looked like a Ferris wheel—except George Ferris didn't build his steam-driven contraption until 1893 in Chicago. This ride was powered by a pulley and a couple of strong men. It had four seats, carried

**Auto racing:
an Ex favourite**

eight passengers, and lifted them 4.6 metres (15 feet) in the air.

The Ex was full of wonders.

## Getting Wired

Some of the wonders were electrifying. The Ex was the first fair in the world to have electric lights. In 1882, 200 arc lamps blazed overhead, seven years after a Toronto man named Henry Woodward took out a patent on his new invention—the electric light bulb. Henry used a carbon filament inside a clear round globe, and lit up the Morrison Brass Company on Adelaide Street for an hour or so. Then he ran out of money and had to sell his patent to a fellow in the United States named Thomas Edison.

Edison showed off a few of his gadgets at the Ex. On September 11, 1888, Governor General Stanley recorded a message of greeting to the American president on the Edison cylinder of the Edison Improved Phonograph. The cylin-

der's still around—and on it is the oldest recorded sound in the world. Toronto also had a look at Edison's "Vitascope" in 1896. It was a movie called *The Kiss*, and it starred a Grimsby girl named May Irwin.

Electric lights dazzled the folks gathered for a big dance on March 10, 1884, when the first free Toronto Public Library opened in the old Mechanics Institute building. On the shelves, ready to be borrowed, were 30,611 books. Five weeks after the dance, the lights shone down upon the naked scalps at the first meeting of the Toronto Baldheaded Men's Club. By 1911 all of Toronto was lit by electricity, and the old lamplighter was out of a job.

**Steam tractor
demonstration at
the CNE**

Even after the telephone arrived in Toronto in the 1880s, you couldn't dial a number. Instead, you turned a crank and an operator—a man until the end of the century, when women were hired because they could be paid less—said, "Number please?" You gave the number and the operator fiddled with plugs and switches until you were connected.

The first electric streetcar in North America, invented by another Torontonian, John Wright, was tried at the Ex too, on September 13, 1883. It used a third rail, just like today's subway system, to carry the juice. (Sixty years later—to the day—the first woman conductor took tickets on the Yonge Street cars.)

The following year, 1884, saw another North American first: the streetcars were outfitted with trolley poles, those things that come off the overhead wires and make drivers swear under their breath. The *Globe* reported with great alarm that the new cars went 15 miles an hour (24 k.p.h.) on curves. This was a little too fast for one American tourist. Charles Zwick, a passenger on a horse-car going the other way, leaned out the window too far and fell in front of the first electric streetcar. He wasn't badly hurt, and he was instantly famous: he was the first person to get hit by a Toronto streetcar, and he's in this book.

By the end of the century electric streetcars ran on most of the major streets in Toronto.

But some people didn't think it was the better way. One of them wrote:

*What will be the result of the trolley's application to King, Queen and Yonge Streets? The trolley will drive off carriages, decrease the value of property and increase danger to life. It is a mistake to accept it and it is a curse when it does come.*

Then the churches got into the act, claiming that Sunday should be held sacred, and that Sunday streetcars were the devil's chariots. Finally, after three votes, a dozen bribes, thunderings from

**Showing off the new electric streetcar at the Ex**

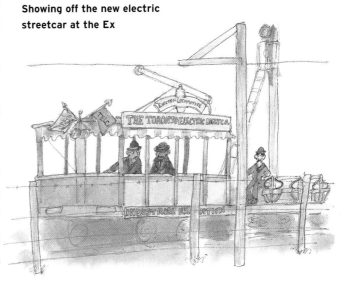

Toronto was—and is—weird about Sunday. The *Globe* was fined $100 in 1895 for putting out a special edition on the Sunday after its offices had burned; a Salvation Army trumpeter was arrested for playing in the park on a Sunday; Sunday tobogganing was outlawed—and a century later, police charged furrier Paul Magder more than 600 times for keeping his store open on Sundays.

the pulpits, fist fights on the City Hall steps, crookedness in high places, and the strange spectacle of the Methodists selling bicycles, the people said yes to Sunday streetcars. For some, Toronto the Good was going bad.

Alexander Graham Bell showed off his gadget too. (He wasn't the first to make a phone, by the way: a German schoolteacher named Philipp Reis made one as a toy in 1861.) Soon Eaton's had one telephone and Simpson's had two. George Brown invested money in Bell's machine but then changed his mind, certain the thing wouldn't catch on.

A few months later Toronto had its first switchboard, connecting 40 telephone owners. By 1887 there were 12,000 telephones in Canada, and ten years after that you could chat with someone 1,200 miles away. Dial phones arrived in 1924. Now, of course, there are all kinds of phones: cordless phones, cell phones, radiophones, antique phones, phones that don't look like phones, and duck-shaped phones that quack instead of ring. We can call anywhere in the world—and we do it a lot.

**For Toronto,** the twentieth century started not with a bang but with a bong. In fact, twelve of them. They came from the three large bells in the clock of the new City Hall. Ten years in the building, made of red rock quarried from the Credit River valley, the City Hall was created by architect Edward Lennox—who carved his own moustached face among the stone gargoyles over the doors, and put Lyon Mackenzie's coat of arms on every doorknob. At midnight on December 31, 1900, from their tower 87 metres (285 feet) above Queen Street, the bells rang out for the first time, announcing the turn of the year. And listening—from the mills on the Humber to the shacks on the Don, from the steamboats in the harbour to the Town Hall in Eglinton—were 200,000 Torontonians, 6,200 hectares (24 square miles) of people.

## The Second Great Fire

A different sound, eerie, urgent, frightening, rang through the streets on the night of April 19, 1904. It was the sound of sirens. Toronto was on fire again.

It was a cold night for April: −5°C. It felt even colder with a 50 k.p.h. (31 m.p.h.) north wind, gusting to 75 k.p.h. (47 m.p.h.). Night watchman Johnson turned up his coat collar as he walked south on Bay Street. At Wellington he smelled smoke. He ran westward and then he saw it: flame billowing from the roof of Currie Neckwear (where the TD Centre is today). He raced to the nearest alarm box, at King and Bay, and smashed the glass. It was four minutes after eight o'clock. And it was already too late: the flames had found the shaft of that marvellous new invention, the elevator, and roared skywards, igniting all four floors on the way.

In the Lombard Street fire hall a few blocks away, Fire Chief John Thompson hastily gulped his tea. Minutes later he was at the blaze, with three fire engines, an aerial truck, a hook-and-ladder truck, and a water tower. He knew immediately that the Currie Building was a goner.

**The morning after, looking up
Bay Street towards City Hall**

But, in a move many thought stupid, he took four men and tried to get to the roof of the six-storey "skyscraper" next door, which housed a fur company, a hat factory, and a soap works. They got to the third floor before smoke stopped them: the skyscraper was on fire all around them. They smashed a window and threw down a rope. The firemen below tied a hose to the rope and it was pulled back up. Then the trapped men, their hands and faces a crazy mix of soot and ice, slid down the hose. The chief slid a bit too fast. His right leg slammed into the new asphalt pavement and snapped. Twenty-six minutes after the start of the biggest fire of his career, Chief Thompson was out of it.

The Great Fire lasted eight hours, the flames leaping tall buildings—and wide streets—in a single bound. Every fire-man in the city was on the scene by nine o'clock; at midnight Hamilton fire-fighters hurtled in on a train to help; more shuffled in from Buffalo at 3:30; and at 5 a.m., in time for breakfast at the just-opened King Edward Hotel, more men came from Brantford, London, Peterborough, and Niagara Falls.

**It was no use.** Building after building was consumed as the flames soared hundreds of metres in the smoky air. Shattered windows, burning bits of eaves-trough, chunks of charred timber rained down in a deadly shower. E.B. Eddy Match Company flared and died; Copp Clark, W.J. Gage, Barber & Ellis Envelopes and Brown Brothers Stationery were four

Early traffic signal – and early traffic cop

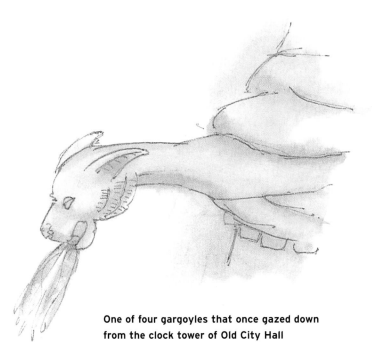

**One of four gargoyles that once gazed down from the clock tower of Old City Hall**

tall poles that carried the wires became giant Roman candles; and every elevator shaft in downtown Toronto, just like the first one at Currie Neckwear, was a perfect wind tunnel.

In spite of 200 firemen and 11 million litres (3 million gallons) of water, 122 buildings—220 businesses—were nothing but charred rubble. Ten million dollars went up in smoke. Eight hectares (20 acres) of downtown Toronto, from Melinda to the waterfront, from York to Yonge Street, were little more than scorched earth.

of 23 book and paper companies turned to ash in minutes; the Eckardt Casket Factory burned down; and the explosion of the Howland warehouse, loaded with cartridges and dynamite, was a rerun of the War of 1812.

And all those marks of progress, all those new inventions, all those improvements, only added to the disaster: the paved streets buckled into huge hummocks and split apart; the mains carrying Consumers' Gas burst open like peapods and threw their contents into the hungry fire; the electric power lines and the telephone wires, heavy with ice, broke and fell, fizzing lethal blue sparks at the firemen and the thousands of spectators who had brought camp chairs and picnic lunches downtown to watch; the

## The Car

The horses that pulled the water carts and engines in the Great Fire were soon seen no more: the car had come to Toronto. More than anything else in its history, the car changed the way the city worked and the way its people lived. And it's still doing so.

1904 to 1929

**From the Car to the Crash**

Toronto really gets wired: note the repairmen atop the tall telephone poles. The shorter poles carry electricity to the streetcars and to the exciting new arc lamps downtown, like the one you see on the corner. Nearby, kids run after one of Toronto's first electric "horseless carriages." Many of the streets and sidewalks are now paved, putting an end to the nickname "Muddy York." This makes it a lot easier to pedal a bike, and thousands of them crowd the downtown streets every day. Then as now, the streetcar tracks were an obstacle course for cyclists. The Coffin Block has been replaced by the Gooderham or Flatiron Building, owned by the descendants of those who built the gristmill on the bay. Toronto has come of age: in 1900 it ranks with New York and London as a splendid example of a Victorian city.

**As** soon as Toronto had cars, Toronto had accidents. One of the first was in 1899 on Jarvis Street. Mr. R. Parker, of Parker's Cleaners—still in business— was driving south when all at once the wheels on one side of his truck just stopped turning. The wheels on the other side didn't. Mr. R. Parker and his truck smashed into the curb. A few years later, the first woman to have an accident— and the first to own a car—was Lady Flora Eaton, John's wife and Timothy's daughter-in-law. She had to call a cab to get home to her huge estate, Ardwold, remembered today in Ardwold Gate north of Casa Loma.

The same year Mr. Parker had his accident, the Canada Cycle & Motor Company—CCM, whose bikes most kids rode for the next 50 years—started up. They made tricycles and quadri-

Electric-car crash
on Glen Road bridge

cycles, which looked like prehistoric dune buggies and were used by the Post Office for mail collection and delivery. Soon they were selling the two-cylinder Russell, a cute little car that sputtered more than it sped. Before long, cars made by Eli Olds, James Packard, and Henry Ford—who turned out a cheapie for $750—jostled for room on the roads. The British-American Oil Company stopped dumping gasoline, which was left over when they made kerosene, into the Don River, and decided to sell it instead.

## The Castle

Henry Pellatt owned a car too, the first electric one in Toronto. On one of his first outings he ran into trouble—or

By 1902, cars were so common that Toronto rewrote its traffic laws. The speed limit was 15 miles (24 km) an hour in the city, unless you were within 100 yards (91 m) of a horse-drawn vehicle, in which case it was 7 miles (11 km) an hour. If your car scared a horse, you had to pull into a side street, park, and go back and calm it down, or be fined $25. You couldn't pass a streetcar with its doors open, either. You still can't.

rather, he ran into a pile of hay. He'd taken the car over to his favourite hangout, the Armoury on University Avenue (where the Court Building is today) to show it off to his favourite regiment, the Queen's Own Rifles. He couldn't get it to stop. It kept going around in circles until the soldiers threw some hay in front of it.

> The victory of Adam Beck over Henry Pellatt—of public ownership over private ownership of things like electricity, streetcars, water, garbage collection, and schools—set Toronto on a course different from that of many big American cities. The people of the city decided that they, rather than a person or company wanting to make a profit, should control the services of the city.

Henry *never* knew when to stop. That's why he was a track star at Upper Canada College in 1875, when he was 16; and why he was a world champ miler in 1879, with a time of 4 minutes 32 seconds. (He ran the last 100 yards in 12 seconds, a record not beaten till 1930.) It is also why he made—and lost—tens of millions of dollars, and why he ended up weighing 135 kilograms (300 pounds).

And it is why he built the craziest landmark in Toronto, the "house on the hill," Casa Loma.

Henry was the first of six children born to a rich Kingston family. When he was two, they moved to Toronto, where his father opened his own brokerage office. Henry left school at 17, and joined the Queen's Own Rifles the next year. He rose to commanding officer of that regiment before he died. But soldiering was more a hobby than a job.

Business—making money—was the love of his life. And he was very good at it. In the 1890s he made a fortune using other people's money to speculate in western land and railways. With this money he bought the Toronto Electric Light Company and sold power to most of the city, including the Toronto Railway Company for its streetcars. Henry and some of his rich buddies wanted to own all the electricity in the province—so they could charge whatever they pleased—but a man named Adam Beck had different ideas. His motto was "Power to the People."

**If Henry knew** how to make money, he also knew how to spend it. And once again he didn't know when to stop. He took all 657 men of his regiment to England to watch Edward VII get crowned, and bought the bugle band new bugles for the trip. He took them to New York, where they wowed the Yanks with precision drills. He handed out medals commemorating the coronation of George V to every girl and boy in Toronto. He collected weapons and armour, some of which was a thousand years old, and then gave it all to the Royal Ontario Museum. He threw parties at the Ex for 10,000 people at a time. And above the shoreline of that ancient glacial lake, just west of Spadina, he built himself a castle.

Casa Loma is both splendid and ridiculous. Designed by Edward Lennox, the same fellow who did the Old City Hall, it cost $3.5 million, and if you count the stables, the deer park, and the greenhouses, it took 10 years to build. The stables were built first: Henry had a band of horses, all with fancy pedigrees, and for them he wanted nothing but the best. The best cost him a quarter of a million dollars. His horses walked on Spanish tiles and slept in mahogany stalls with 18-karat-gold nameplates. For his pet horse, Prince, Henry bought a set of porcelain false teeth.

The stables were joined to the castle basement by a 244-metre (800-foot) tunnel. Near the tunnel entrance was an enormous furnace, which burned 725 tons of coal—that's 1,600,000 pounds, or 725,000 kilograms—every winter. Just to make sure everybody kept warm, Henry added 25 fireplaces. There was a stove in the kitchen you could roast a cow in.

There were 98 rooms and 30 bathrooms. There were 5,000 electric lights. There was an elevator; an indoor swimming pool; a built-in vacuum cleaning system (the vacuum cleaner had just been invented in 1908); a fountain; a dozen or so telephones; a shooting gallery for his army buddies; and three—count 'em, three—alleys for the brand-new game of five-pin bowling, invented a couple of years earlier by Torontonian Tommy Ryan. The whole place was crammed with tapestries and paintings and sculpture and furniture and carpets and crystal and silver and general loot from almost every country in the world.

In the front hall was a throne and a $75,000 pipe organ. In Henry's library were 100,000 books. The stone wall that still surrounds the castle was built by Welsh and Scottish masons, brought across the Atlantic to do the job. Each

Casa Loma, "The House on the Hill"

Henry Pellatt and his wife, Mary, a Bishop Strachan "Old Girl," threw unbelievable parties. He invited a thousand soldiers over for the weekend; she, as Commissioner of Girl Guides, had 500 girls to lunch. Hordes of the "beautiful people" of two continents regularly drank tea or other stronger brews in the conservatory, or sauntered in the gardens, where 400 kinds of trees and shrubs grew.

stone cost Henry a dollar. Each mason cost him a dollar a day.

**It couldn't last.** Henry kept borrowing money for new and riskier ideas, or just to have in his pockets in case he wanted to buy a toy—and he had bigger pockets than anybody. One by one, all his companies went bankrupt. In 1923, the Home Bank—which had loaned him most of the money—failed, and many ordinary people lost all their savings. There was a scandal, Mary died of a heart attack, and Henry was nearly broke.

Casa Loma and everything in it had to go. The city bought the buildings for $27,305.45, the amount owing in back taxes. The Persian rugs sold for the price of doormats. Henry's million-dollar art collection was picked up at Honest Ed prices. Five solid silver spoons and a gravy ladle, once owned by John Simcoe, were bought for $28 by an American,

which John wouldn't have liked at all. A lucky fellow named Franklin got the $75,000 organ for $40. Henry stayed for a while at his 600-acre (243 hectare) farm in King, but soon that too was sold, as was a house at 78 Crescent Road. On his eightieth birthday some friends had a party for him, and the old bugle corps of the Queen's Own Rifles, for whom he'd bought those shiny new instruments, shuffled in to play him a tune. He died in 1939 at 28 Queens Drive in Mimico, in a house so tiny he could have put it in a corner of Casa Loma's front hall. With him was Thomas Ridgeway, his chauffeur, valet, and perhaps last friend.

Now, half a million people pay to visit Henry's castle every year. The Kiwanis Club runs the place and the money goes to help children. It's still splendid. It's still ridiculous. Even kids who live thousands of kilometres away know about Casa Loma. They've read about it in a poem by Dennis Lee called "The Cat and the Wizard":

> In Casa Loma
> Lives a cat
> With a jet-black coat
> And a tall silk hat ...

or in the book by Eric Wilson, *The Lost Treasure of Casa Loma*. Henry would have been pleased.

## Sports and Spectacles

Watching the castle take shape was a popular hobby, but there were others too:

### Football

In 1909, Governor General Earl Grey, also famous for his tea, offered a silver cup to the best football team in Canada. The Toronto Argonauts, formed in 1874 and still going, didn't make the playoffs, but two other Toronto teams did: the University of Toronto won 26–6 over Toronto Parkdale Canoe Club. Those were the days when the forward pass, the "huddle," hiring Americans, and paying the players hadn't even been thought of.

### Hockey

In 1908, with the formation of the Ontario Professional League, Canada's most popular sport turned pro. The name of the game comes from the French word *hoquet*, a shepherd's crook, which the stick resembles. Popular since the 1850s, when it was played with a round ball on any handy patch of ice, the first true hockey game took place in Montreal in 1875, with rules devised by a college student and a flat wooden disc instead of a ball. It caught on all over the continent.

### Horse Races

In 1908 the Dufferin Park Race Track opened. Dufferin was the first track to use a starting gate and the first to use a camera to help the judges pick a winner in close finishes.

Toronto amateur hockey teams won the gold in the 1924 and 1928 Olympics, but the glory days of the city's pro team, the Maple Leafs, were still to come. In the 1940s, with superstars Turk Broda, Syl Apps, and Ted Kennedy, Toronto's Leafs would capture the Stanley Cup six times in 10 years.

### Human Races

In 1906 a horse ran a poor second in a 12-mile (19.3 km) race against Tom Longboat, one of the greatest long-distance runners who ever lived. Tom was born in 1887 on the Six Nations Reserve in Brantford but spent most of his life in Toronto. He first got into the news in 1906 when he won the oldest race in North America, the 19-mile (31 km) Hamilton "Around-the-Bay" run. The following year, with the Las Vegas bookies laying odds against him of 60 to 1, he easily led the field in the Boston Marathon, running 25 miles (40 km) in a record-breaking 2 hours 25 minutes and one-fifth of a second. Toronto gave him a huge welcome, a parade, a flag, and a medal.

Thomas Charles Longboat of the Onondaga nation, Canada's greatest long-distance runner

During World War I, Tom Longboat ran all over France as an army messenger. When he returned to Toronto for the second time, there was no parade, no flag, no medal, no welcome. There was only a job as a street cleaner for the former champion runner. Tom died in 1949, poor and almost forgotten, never knowing that a Scarborough school would one day bear his name.

## Parades

December 2, 1905, was a great day for Toronto's children. Chugging into the old three-towered, cave-like Union Station, straight from the North Pole, came a train carrying Santa Claus, about to star in his first parade. Sponsored by Eaton's—as it was for the next 76 years—the parade had only a few horse-drawn wagons. They made their way north to the Eaton's store, where Santa settled in to be sat upon by hordes of kids, all wanting the toys in the Christmas catalogue: a baseball bat and a catcher's mitt for 79 cents; a musical top for a quarter; or a "Teddy Bear," a new toy named after U.S. president Teddy Roosevelt, who once spared a bear cub's life while on a hunting trip.

Another favourite parade was the Orangemen's Parade, which took place every July 12. The Orangemen were members of the Grand Orange Lodge of British North America, a Protestant club with secret handshakes, often violent anti-Catholic feeling, and a lot of political power in the years 1850–1925. (For decades, nobody got a job at city hall unless they were "Orange.") July 12 marked the anniversary of the Battle of the Boyne in 1690, when the Protestant King William of Orange beat the Catholic King James II. It's a kind of Protestant St. Patrick's Day. The parade was spectacular, with a dozen bands, thousands of marchers wearing orange banners and orange tiger lilies (planted so they'd bloom July 11), and someone dressed as "King Billy" riding the biggest white horse in the city. The parade ended at the Exhibition grounds with an enormous picnic, and everybody except the Catholics went.

### Flying Machines

In 1908, at Scarborough Beach, American pilot Charles Willard showed off the first airplane most Torontonians had ever seen. On his first try he flew 90 metres (300 feet), then dropped into the lake. On his second try he flew for almost five minutes, had no room to land, and dropped into the lake. On his third try his generator conked out. He dropped into the lake. Willard later got into the history books as the first pilot to be shot down. A farmer sent a few bullets into his machine when he flew a little too low over a herd of cows.

### Flying Insects

Airplanes weren't the only things that fell to earth. In 1912, the *Daily Star*, a newspaper started in 1893 by a group of printers locked out by their bosses, and famous for its flashy style, sponsored a six-week fly-swatting contest. All kids under age 16 could enter, and 66 did. The total number of swatted flies, which were stored in bottles supplied by the Department of Health, was 3,367,680. They weighed 596.7 kilograms (1,316 pounds).

### Melodrama and Diorama

Both the Royal Alexandra Theatre and the Royal Ontario Museum opened their fancy doors in this peaceful time. The people of Toronto flocked to one to hear, live from New York, Al Jolson sing "My Mammy," and to the second to see, dead from Egypt, mummies of the ancient Pharaohs. Now that Honest Ed Mirvish owns the Alex—he saved it from the wreckers in 1963 and fixed it up the way it once was—its 1,500 seats are filled every night, and every year more than half a million people visit the ROM, the largest museum in Canada.

In 1912, Beatrice White became the Queen of Swat in the *Star's* fly-swatting contest, winning $50 for downing 543,360 flies. This works out to one cent for every 109 flies.

**In the social notices** of 1914 were two items of special interest. The first reported the death of John McLaughlin, the man who made Canada Dry ginger ale. John started small, selling bottles of mineral water. By 1894 he had a plant on Sherbourne Street, where 10 years later he began to make what he called "dry ginger ale." Soon Canada Dry was sold in dozens of countries around the world.

The second item said that Marshall

Saunders had moved into the house at 62 Glengowan Road. She wrote *Beautiful Joe*, the first Canadian book to sell more than a million copies. It's a dog story guaranteed to make you cry, and you can still borrow it from the library or buy it at a bookstore.

In August 1914 the peaceful years came to an end. Canada was at war.

**Saying goodbye,
1914-1918**

1914 marked the birth of Joe Shuster, who, at age 17, created Superman. Shuster's first *Superman* comic featured the mild-mannered reporter Clark Kent working at the *Daily Star*, which later on became the *Daily Planet*. The city of Metropolis was based on Toronto. Joe was definitely not a good businessman: he sold the strip—and the character—for $130.

## The Carnage

At first the lines were long in front of the Armoury. In two weeks, 927 men enlisted. Everyone thought the war would be over in a month, and the young men and boys who rushed to join the army, or the navy, or the Royal Flying Corps, were afraid they'd miss the action. They needn't have worried.

Then the lists of the dead and wounded began to arrive. They were long. They were as long as the lines in front of the Armoury. And they kept coming.

Seventy thousand young men, more than a seventh of Toronto's population, left the city for the mud and blood of Europe. Thirteen thousand didn't come back. Of those that did, many thousands were crippled, or maimed, or sick from mustard and chlorine gas. But many thousands were saved, too, by an army doctor from Toronto named George

Nasmith. When the first gas attacks came, he quickly put together a pad soaked with a soda compound to absorb the chlorine. It was the world's first gas mask. We owe our water purification system to the same man: in 1910, when 151 Torontonians died of typhoid fever, a disease caused by dirty water or food, he insisted that the city filter and treat its water.

Toronto settled in to win the war. Soldiers camped at the Ex and on the playing fields of the university. Pilots learned how to fly in Long Branch and Armour Heights and Leaside. The Flying Jennies—Curtiss JNs—they learned on (and sometimes died in: in the last year of the war 125 cadets and instructors were killed in crashes) were made by the Canadian Aeroplane Company at Dufferin and Lappin streets. Work went on around the clock, 24 hours a day, and

During the war, Eaton's paid the wages of enlisted married men to their families, paid enlisted single men half their salary, and, every year of the war, sent a Christmas box to each overseas employee. This all cost the company $2 million before the war was over.

Christie-Brown Cookies paid the wages of all their workers who joined up, and guaranteed them jobs when (or if) they returned.

Neilson gave 65,000 chocolate bars to the soldiers.

2,900 trainer-planes were built. Toronto became the centre of the aviation industry.

Gooderham & Worts, whose ancestors had built that first windmill, and whose whisky had supplied the world, donated their factories and mills down on the waterfront to make acetone, which was used in explosives.

Massey, now Massey-Harris after an 1891 merger, wasn't so generous. Because of lost sales in Europe, they shut down the factory and laid off 1,500 men. Then they realized they could make a killing, so to speak, in munitions. They opened up again to make 8.2-kilogram (18-pound) cannon shells. On one order of 100,000 shells they made a profit of $400,000. Nothing like beating your ploughshares into swords.

The big textile and clothing firms in the Spadina and Queen area, where

The army shows off its new war machine to raise money.

**Mourning mothers in the Warriors' Day Parade at the Ex, soon after World War I**

thousands of Jewish immigrants worked after fleeing from persecution in eastern Europe, geared up to make uniforms and blankets and tents.

Women went out to work, in huge numbers, making cannons and bullets and seaplanes, doing the jobs of the men who had gone overseas—at half the pay. (Then they went home and did all the housework.) Women finally got the vote, too, for provincial elections in 1916 and for federal elections two years later. Two women who helped bring this about were Emily Stowe, the first woman doctor in Canada, and her daughter Augusta Stowe-Gullen, the first woman to be allowed into Toronto Medical School. You can go and see her house at 461 Spadina Road. They also paved the way for the beginnings of Women's College Hospital in 1910.

And Mayor Tommy Church was everywhere, saying goodbye to the sol-diers as they boarded the trains at Union Station, greeting them by name when they came home again, and visiting the families of those who didn't come home.

**After four years** of savagery and sorrow, on the morning of November 11, 1918, Mayor Church ordered a steam whistle to blast from the City Hall tower. The people of Toronto ran into the streets, shouting and crying and beating pots and pans and washtubs. Miles of ticker tape rained from the high windows on Bay Street. Women threw talcum powder and kisses. And through all the city there was a great and joyful noise. The war was over.

**On the medical front,** a young doctor, back from the trenches with a wound in his arm and a medal on his chest, got an idea. Scientists had suspected for some time that the human pancreas sent a hormone into the bloodstream to help the body use sugar. But they weren't sure, and even if such a hormone existed, they didn't know how to get hold of it. The young doctor's name was Frederick Banting, and his idea, though not quite on the right track, eventually led to the discovery of insulin, the "miracle" treatment for diabetes.

A team of scientists—including tal-ented researcher Charles Best—did the work at the University of Toronto. The team's head man was John MacLeod, and he and Banting shared the Nobel Prize for medicine in 1923. Banting immediately gave half of his prize money to Best, calling him the co-discoverer of insulin.

The first person to be treated with insulin was a dying 14-year-old boy named Leonard Thompson. His life was saved. Hundreds of thousands of lives have been saved since. Fred Banting's life was lost early, however: en route to Britain in 1941, his plane crashed near Musgrave Harbour in Newfoundland.

## Let the Good Times Roll

After the war, after the death and destruction and disillusion, after the unspeakable grief, people went a little wacky. They wanted fun.

In Toronto, we danced. We danced shocking dances with strange names: the Black Bottom, where hands gripped hips; the Butterfly, in which kicking heels and flapping hands nearly made you airborne; the Bunny Hop, which was just the way it sounds; the Strut, where you were so close to your partner you looked like one body; the Shimmy, in which you shook your top and your middle and your bottom; and the most famous, the most frantic, the most fatiguing of all, the Charleston.

Even though an armistice was declared in November 1918, the deaths were not over. In the last year of the war a pandemic of flu raged through most of the world. Starting in Spain, it spread through Europe and then came to North America with the returning soldiers. Before it was over, nearly 22 million people were dead, more than twice the number who had been killed in the war. In Toronto, schools and factories and offices were closed, but still there were 1,259 deaths, the worst plague since the cholera epidemics of the nineteenth century.

We danced at the Masonic Temple at Davenport and Yonge; at Tichener Smith's Studio, a half-block south of the spot where, a hundred years before, the young had waltzed in the Red Lion Inn; at Dean's Boathouse, later called the

Bumper cars, a favourite ride at Sunnyside

**The crowds at Sunnyside**

Palais Royale, on the lakeshore. And when, in 1928, the Royal York was built where the stately old Queen's Hotel had been, we dressed up in tuxedos and skin-tight gowns and danced in its ballroom.

We went to Sunnyside Amusement Park, which opened in 1922. There was a fish pond, a Ferris wheel, a roller coaster, and a merry-go-round (whose horses now grace King Arthur's Carousel at Disneyland in California). There were games of skill, of strength, of chance, where you could win a celluloid doll no bigger than your finger, or a set of dishes, or a bamboo cane with a toy monkey tied to it, all of which broke on the way home.

Toronto's own George Young beat the world's best swimmers in the Wrigley Marathon of 1927. Seventeen-year-old George walked naked and shivering onto a California beach after 15 hours and 46 minutes in the water. He had swum 30 miles (48 km) through waves, changing tides, seaweed, and a couple of curious sharks—and he was the only swimmer to finish the course. When he came home, we had—what else?— a parade.

There were hot dogs for a dime, mountainous ice cream sundaes for a quarter, and pink candy floss for a nickel. And on Easter Sunday—in rain or snow or gale-force wind—we showed off our new spring clothes on the boardwalk.

There was a huge swimming pool at Sunnyside too, which was proudly called the "outdoor natatorium" but was known to all the kids as the "tank." It could hold 2,000 bodies—and it usually did—and the smell of chlorine nearly knocked you out. Kids got a free ride to the pool on a special TTC "bathing car." If you couldn't afford the 10 cents for the pool, you went to the beach, miles and miles of it, and tried to find a spot to sunbathe. Most of the beach was covered with people. Most of your body was covered too. Girls wore roomy overblouses and long wool shorts,

and if young men bared their chests, they were arrested—except for the marathon swimmers, some of whom wore only grease.

We listened, awestruck, to a new machine called a radio. When you slide your earphones on today, you're doing what your great-grandparents did in 1922. The first radios were called crystal sets, not much more than a bunch of lead sulfur crystals with wires attached. They picked up a faint whisper of sound from the general direction of King Street, where CFCA, the city's first radio station, owned by the *Daily Star*, was located. One of the first voices we heard was that of a young reporter named Foster Hewitt,

Maskless goalie Johnny Bower, one of the Maple Leaf greats

**Young hockey fans listen to the game.**

giving us a play-by-play of the Maple Leafs hockey game in Mutual Street Arena. Later, in 1931, when Maple Leaf Gardens was built in an astonishing 5 months and 12 days, we heard the same voice say, "He shoots! He scores!"—as we would for the next fifty years.

It wasn't long before battery-run radios were on the market. The batteries weren't the little thumb-sized ones you use today. These batteries were bigger than breadboxes, and so, of course, were the radios they ran. It was a man from Toronto who changed all that.

Ted Rogers was born on the first day of summer in 1900. He tinkered with electricity as a boy, and when he was 13, he won a prize for the best-built radio in Ontario. At age 21 he was the only Canadian to win in a North American contest to broadcast across the ocean. And three years later he made a radio you could plug into the wall. His invention revolutionized the entire industry. He founded the Rogers Majestic Radio Company, and in 1927 his radio station went on the air. CFRB—the last two letters stand for "Rogers Batteryless"—is still going strong. Ted was busy with further marvels—television and radar—when he died suddenly just before his thirty-ninth birthday. But the company he founded is still alive and thriving.

Early programs were local and amateur. One of the first, in 1923, was a reading, chapter by chapter by chapter, of Charles Dickens's *The Old Curiosity Shop*. Another was a broadcast of the pit orchestra at the Uptown Theatre on Yonge Street, a block from Bloor. The Uptown showed some of the first "talkie" movies, including one called *Mother Knows Best*, in which Mother died at the end. The people who looked after the mikes hadn't quite got the hang of them, and when Mom rattled out her last breath, you could hear her all the way up to Bloor.

Meanwhile, farther south at the huge Shea's Hippodrome Theatre below City Hall, the kids lined up to see *The Phantom of the Opera*, a scary film made even scar-ier by being silent.

## Blind Pigs and Bullets

The ten years after the war were called the Roaring Twenties, and Toronto roared as much as its dignity allowed. But the roar was muffled a little by a law passed in 1916 called the Ontario Temperance Act, which abolished bars, clubs, and liquor stores. You could buy liquor only with a doctor's prescription. Not surprisingly, a lot of people immediately got diseases that only liquor could cure. One doctor wrote 487 prescriptions in a day. If we assume he worked an eight-hour day, he must have handed out one prescription every minute—at two dollars apiece.

You could also buy alcohol, illegally, in places called "blind pigs." The name comes from a tricky nineteenth-century Massachusetts innkeeper. At that time, the law was strict about selling liquor, so he let it be known that for a small fee—about the price of a drink—customers could view an amazing striped pig. Once they paid, they were led to a hidden, or "blind," alcove where they found a clay model of a striped pig—and a glass of rum.

We had our own gangs of bootleggers. They'd load up their cars and trucks and boats at Gooderham & Worts (back making whisky after the war) and run across to Buffalo and Fort Erie and Niagara Falls with cases of booze to sell to the thirsty Yanks, who suffered under their own Prohibition law.

We even had a gunfight in Ashbridge's Bay, that peaceful stretch of water known to Sara Ashbridge and her sons 130 years before. A young man named John Gogo, delivering 2,500 quarts (2,370 l) of whisky to Rocco Perri, the king of Ontario bootleggers, was shot in the chest by Toronto police. In a couple of minutes Gogo was a goner.

Eventually, people realized it was a stupid law. It hadn't done much except make a few gangsters and brewers very rich and everybody else mad. In 1927 it was repealed.

## Wasps on the Wane

Toronto went back to having fun. And there were more of us to have fun. In the

Toronto had self-appointed "Dry Squads" during Prohibition. Members were often clergymen. These squads raided hotels and even private homes to smash liquor bottles and heads. A Methodist minister actually shot and killed a hotel owner in Windsor. He was tried for manslaughter and acquitted.

first 30 years of this century the number of people living in Toronto more than tripled, to 631,000. There were also more kinds of people: these were the years we began to be less British.

Tens of thousands of people came from all over the world: Poles and Ukrainians to work in the stockyards and meat-packing plants at the junction of Keele and Dundas streets; Jews from Russia and eastern Europe to open Kensington Market in 1905 and a tiny drugstore on Elizabeth Street in 1909, which grew up to be Mount Sinai Hospital, and to settle in the streets

**Six boys find a great toy at Davenport and Bathurst, then the suburbs. Many short lines – and the cars that ran on them – were abandoned when the TTC took over in 1923.**

After World War I, there were more people in the streets and more streets for people to be in. The viaduct over the Don, finished in 1918, joined Danforth to Bloor and brought a huge rush of growth to east Toronto.

nearby; Macedonians and Greeks to live and work near the railroad at Eastern Avenue; Italians, following in the footsteps of their countryman Philippe De Grassi so many years before, to build the streets and bridges and houses and hotels of the city; blacks from the Caribbean to live near Front and Sherbourne, and attend the First Baptist Church, founded in 1826 by runaway slaves and still on Huron Street, where it began; and Chinese, who drifted eastward after building the railways through the Rockies, to open laundries and restaurants and stores and newspapers and theatres near the Grange, the old home of D'Arcy Boulton.

**Streets were cleared** and paved. Houses sprang up. If you didn't mind transferring half a dozen times, you could ride all over Toronto on the streetcars and trolley buses; there were more of those too. And you could also visit the 200,000 people who lived in the villages on Toronto's borders—villages that, 30 years later, would become part of the greater city of Metro Toronto: Leaside, East York, Mimico, New Toronto, Long Branch, Forest Hill, Weston, and Swansea.

But the folks walking and riding the streets of Toronto weren't young people. In 1921 a new law was passed, the Adolescent Attendance Act. Kids now had to go to school until they were 16. This meant that more secondary schools were needed. Some city council members didn't like this. They said secondary schools weren't necessary. They said kids would become spoiled and soft and unfit for the world of work. They said that half the things the Board of Education spent money on were "fads and frills"—such as kindergarten, music, art, and free workbooks and readers.

## The Crash

The city was busy and getting busier, rich and getting richer, big and getting bigger. Most people had jobs, most families had a decent place to live, most kids had plenty to eat. In 1929, Toronto was happy, hopeful, and harmonious—right up until October 29, a day known ever after as "Black Tuesday." After 10 years of wild spending and wilder stock speculation—where company shares are bought and sold at prices way above their real value—the stock market crashed. Like Wall Street in New York, Toronto's Bay Street was a river of useless paper. Businesses went bankrupt; offices closed their doors; stores boarded up their windows; factories locked their gates.

The Dirty Thirties had come to Toronto.

## Hard Times

A year after the crash, nearly a fifth of Toronto working people had no jobs. Two years later, one in three was out of work. And remember: there was no employment insurance, no family allowance, no medical plan, no government welfare. The city council tried to help, giving out food or vouchers for food and rent and fuel, but in the whole ten years of the Depression they never quite got the hang of it. Soon one Torontonian in four had to exist on handouts from the city. In the suburbs it was worse: half of Leaside was "on relief."

**CHAPTER
ONE**

# 1929 to
# 1954

## Want, War, Weather — and the Welcome Mat

The horse and wagon is still around, but cars now rule the roads. There's an early Gray Coach in the middle foreground, and coming around the corner is a camper, probably the only home some people had in the hard years of the Great Depression. Electric lights now line the streets, and wooden streetcars run all over town. The financial district—centred around the Stock Exchange at Leader Lane and Wellington in the upper left—is not a happy place in 1930.

**Long** lines of hungry people formed in front of relief offices, soup kitchens, churches, and the badly named House of Industry—no more than a poorhouse since 1848—on Elm Street. The old library, where hundreds had partied so elegantly 50 years before, was turned into a clothing depot, and tired mothers searched through piles of other people's used clothes to find, if they were lucky, matching mittens and boots for their kids.

It was a time when families fell apart. Children were sent to more prosperous kin or, sadly, to foster parents, or to work as servants in the homes of the rich. Fathers went in search of work and never came back. Some mothers ran away; some fell ill and died; some struggled on, often giving up all they owned—including their pride—to keep their children fed. After a boy reached 16, he was cut off relief. Many of them left home to

The Dirty Thirties was a time when families came together, when your house—if you had a house—was full of relatives. Aunts and uncles and cousins by the dozens, grandmothers and grandfathers, all who lost their homes or who couldn't pay their rent, came to stay. In many parts of Toronto this was against the law—so people broke the law.

wander the continent. They lived in hobo jungles like those at Keele and St. Clair and in the Don Valley, boiling tea or cooking a stolen chicken over an open fire (just as Elizabeth Simcoe and the kids had roasted deer meat 140 years earlier). They begged at back doors until they were run out of town or thrown in jail, where they got a good breakfast after moving bricks from point A to point B—a pointless task—and then they were run out of town again. They "rode the rods"—stole a ride in an empty freight car—until they froze to death, or fell under the wheels, or got kicked in the kidneys by the "yard bulls" (the railway police). Many of them ended up in a "slave camp" run by the army in northern Ontario, making 20 cents a day cutting trees.

It was a time when tired men in grimy clothes, with cardboard insoles in their shoes, spooned up watery soup at the Fred Victor Mission or slept in narrow steel bunks in the stinking flophouse that had once been St. Lawrence Hall.

It was a time when kids dragged wagons along the railroad tracks that criss-crossed the town, looking for stray lumps of coal. And they stopped playing "Chopsticks" on their Heintzman pianos, chopping the instruments into sticks for the stove instead.

It was a time when jobless fathers

The thirties was a time when, if you were lucky enough to have six cents or three empty pop bottles to cash in, you could go to the movies on Saturday afternoon and see *Frankenstein*, *Tarzan of the Apes*, the *News of the World*, a preview of "Coming Attractions," a Mickey Mouse cartoon, and the latest cliff-hanger adventure in an endless sci-fi serial starring Flash Gordon and Emperor Ming of the planet Mongo. And then you could see it all again—for free.

and angry mothers marched to City Hall and Queen's Park to ask for help—until mounted police galloped through the crowds with nightsticks flailing.

It was a time when Prime Minister William Lyon Mackenzie King, a century after his rebel grandfather had protested against the government, sent thousands of protesters to jail or out of the country—and refused to let the Jews of Europe, fleeing from certain death, into the country.

It was a time when signs went up at Balmy Beach and Kew Beach that read "No Jews, Niggers, or Dogs," and brown-shirted thugs shouting "Heil Hitler"—a terrible echo of the shouts 6,000 kilometres away in Germany— paraded on Queen Street and attacked Jews in Christie Pits. (The Jews fought back—and won.)

It was a time when you had your water turned off without notice, your hydro cut off without warning, and your furniture taken to pay back rent— or tumbled onto the sidewalk as you were turned out of your house.

It was a time when you scooped stale bread from the big bins behind Mr. Christie's on King Street, and begged bags of crusts from Diana Sweets on Yonge Street and Muirhead's Cafeteria near Massey Hall, which you then took home to dunk in your potato soup.

It was a time when you yanked the vacuum tubes out of your radio and hid them when the radio licence inspector knocked on your door to collect the three-dollar fee, telling him that the radio didn't work.

It was a time when the rich got poorer and the poor got desperate.

It was the Dirty Thirties.

**Children scavenging for coal**

**But it wasn't all gloom.** After the inspector left, you stuck the tubes back in the radio and listened to *Pepper Young's Family* and *Ma Perkins*, two of the first soap operas; laughed at Fred Allen and Jack Benny and *Amos 'n' Andy*; and scared yourself deliciously with *Fu Manchu* and *The Shadow* and *Inner Sanctum*. You kept happy with Toronto's own *The Happy Gang*; you sent away for a Secret Code Ring from *Little Orphan Annie*. You cheered when the Leafs took the Stanley Cup in three straight from the New York Rangers. And on May 15, 1935, you heard the world's first radio quiz show, *Professor Dick and His Question Box*, invented in Toronto by ex-teacher Roy Ward Dickson. And for a while you'd forget the Dirty Thirties.

It was a time when you could pretend you were a millionaire as you bought Park Plaza, the Boardwalk, and all the railroads in the new game Monopoly, invented by Charles Darrow of Massachusetts. Charles was flat broke at the time. He soon wasn't: tens of millions of sets have been sold so far.

It was a time when you could pretend you were hockey player "King" Clancy or "Hap" Day, as you pulled levers on the new game sensation Table Hockey, invented in 1932 by an out-of-work Toronto man named Don Munro to amuse his children. Sales took off at Eaton's Toyland and the whole Munro family got busy, with Mrs. Munro crocheting the nets and the three kids painting the tiny players.

For some it was the worst of times; for others, the best of times. Both are remembered by Toronto writer Bernice Thurman Hunter in her "Booky" stories.

**The British airship R-100 flies by the Bank of Commerce skyscraper in 1930.**

## Happy Birthday

One of the best times was Toronto's 100th birthday, in 1934. As the City Hall clock tolled midnight on March 6, a rocket zoomed skywards from the beach near the Ex where the Simcoes had stepped ashore. On Gibraltar Point, 200 barrels of tar and resin were set on fire, and a hundred rockets went off, one every 15 seconds, while thousands of Torontonians looked on. The party went on for months, marked by pageants at a spruced-up Fort York, the return of our first mace (swiped by the Yanks back in 1813), and a dazzling air show.

Mary Pickford came to the party. Born Gladys Smith in a little brick house on University Avenue near College Street in 1893, "Baby Gladys" was on Toronto stages at age five, earning enough to feed her widowed mother and her little brother and sister. She'd gone off to Hollywood as a young girl, changed her name, was the first movie star ever, picked up the nickname "America's Sweetheart," married Douglas Fairbanks, founded United Artists film company, and made a million dollars before she was 20.

Lyon Mackenzie's grandson came to the party. So did the descendants of John Simcoe and of the French governor who'd built Fort Rouillé. There were plays about Toronto, poems about Toronto, songs about Toronto. There was a week-long concert at Massey Hall. Led by the soon to be knighted Ernest MacMillan—who now has a school named for him—the Toronto Conservatory Choir sang and the Toronto Symphony Orchestra played, to wild applause and a dozen curtain calls. It was a great bash.

**Cow almost creamed**

## Hot News and Tot News

The second week in July 1936 was the hottest on record, with the temperature hitting over 105°F (41°C) on July 10. It was so hot that people slept in their basements and backyards and bathtubs, in the 38 city parks, on the beaches, on the Islands. It was so hot you could fry an egg on the sidewalk—and somebody did, right on the steps of City Hall. It was so hot you could die—and dozens did. The *Star*'s front page listed the deaths, just as it had in the war to end all wars, just as it soon would again.

It also listed the names of those born in the Millar Stork Derby. Charles Vance Millar, who had died in 1926, was a rich Toronto lawyer with a weird sense of humour. In his will he'd left half a million dollars to the Toronto mother who gave birth to the most children by Halloween of 1936. The woman who should have won, with ten kids in ten years, was disqualified because only five of the children were her husband's and she didn't seem too sure who had fathered the others. The whole crazy scheme ended in fights and court cases. The lawyers made a fortune and the newspapers had a wonderful time. Finally, four women who'd had nine children each split the loot.

Before the polio epidemic of 1937 was over, 758 Torontonians, most of them children, had caught it. Most of those were whisked away to isolation hospitals, where even their parents couldn't visit. Thirty-one died, and many children were paralyzed forever, doomed to spend their life in an "iron lung," a big tank that enclosed their body and helped them breathe.

**Those children,** and all the others in the city, got an unexpected holiday the next year. School didn't start until October 5. The beaches were closed, the swimming pools were closed, and hardly anybody went to the Ex (although a couple of American tourists showed up

The famous — and later famously unhappy — Dionne Quintuplets, Annette, Marie, Émilie, Yvonne, and Cécile, born May 28, 1934. They were taken from their parents and put on display by the provincial government.

carrying gas masks). Kids stayed away from movie theatres and parks and playgrounds and other kids. If you saw two or three people coming your way on the sidewalk, you crossed the street. Mostly, you stayed right in your own backyard—if you had a backyard.

An epidemic of the dreaded and mysterious "infantile paralysis"—polio to you and me—had engulfed the city.

The Salk vaccine—the polio shot—was 18 years in the future. There was no way to prevent the disease. People tried, though. They prayed and they sprayed. They held city-wide prayer meetings asking for divine protection and/or cool weather. It didn't work. And, in a peculiar experiment, they sprayed the noses of 5,000 kids with zinc sulphate, which is the stuff in deodorant that makes your armpits dry up. That didn't work either.

Around the same time, another experiment was a big success: three doctors at the Hospital for Sick Children, including Dr. Alan Brown, who tended the Dionne Quintuplets, cooked up a new cereal for babies. Its name, in every sense and in every city in the world, is a household word: Pablum.

## The King and Queen on King and Queen

Children got another holiday two years later, in 1939, but for a happier reason. King George VI and Queen Elizabeth dropped by, the first time a reigning monarch had ever visited. Everybody who owned a flag hung it, waved it, or wore it. The royal blue royal train, with a crown on its front and a flag on its back, steamed into the North Toronto station—near the spot where Lyon Mackenzie had fired on the soldiers of another queen, and where a liquor store is today—at 10:30 in the morning on May 22, and steamed out of Union Station at 6:30 that night. In eight non-stop hours of smiling ceremony, the royal twosome, with Prime Minister King bowing and scraping behind them, went to: City Hall to salute the cenotaph; Queen's Park, where Cécile Dionne gave the Queen an unexpected hug; the university, to give the Toronto Scottish Regiment a new flag; Riverdale Park, to see 75,000 kids and 100,000 adults, a third of the population of Toronto; Woodbine Race Track for the

During the royal tour of 1939, the King and Queen stayed too long at a hospital, which put them behind schedule in their planned drive around the city. The royal chauffeur had to step on the gas. So, when the big moment came, the throngs lining the route saw only a few motorcycle cops, a couple of shiny cars whizzing past, and two figures that looked like mannequins out of an Eaton's window.

running of the King's Plate; and Christie Street Hospital (where an old folks' home is today, just above the tracks near Dupont) to see 2,000 Great War vets and scores of "Silver Cross" mothers, whose sons had died in the war and who got medals as a reward.

## The Carnage, Part II

Three months later the flags waved again. But nobody smiled. On September 3, Adolf Hitler, the leader of Nazi Germany, plunged the world into war.

Toronto geared up for battle. A thousand men were sworn in during the first weekend of the war. Two of the regiments mustering at the Armoury were Sir Henry Pellatt's favourite, the Queen's Own Rifles, and the Toronto Scottish with their brand-new flag. Soon Stuart, the son of writer L.M. Montgomery—who then lived at 210A Riverside Drive, beside the Humber—would put on the uniform of a navy doctor and say goodbye to his famous mother.

When World War II was declared, there were suddenly lots of jobs. Men who'd been out of work for 10 years either joined the armed forces or had their pick of half a dozen jobs. Women were urged to go to work in war plants. The nightmare of the Depression lifted.

A woman's work was never done.

The horror came closer to home a week later. A special bulletin interrupted Sunday night radio programs in mid-sentence: the passenger ship *Athenia*, with 120 Torontonians aboard, had been torpedoed by a German submarine.

**Just as they** had 25 years earlier, factories switched from making the products of peace to making the machines of war. De Havilland Aircraft grew from a dozen employees to 8,000, and by the war's end had made nearly 3,000 airplanes. A thousand of these were Mosquito bombers, which some experts say won the air war. Massey-Harris stopped making tractors and threshers and binders, and made the wings for those Mosquitos instead. On historic Strachan Avenue, at the John Inglis Company, 17,000 workers—mostly

During the war, 8,000 boys and girls from the British Isles came to Canada, many of them to Toronto, to escape the bombing in their homeland. For many it was a sad time. Alone, living among strangers, teased by their classmates for the way they talked and dressed, worried about their mothers and fathers across the ocean, they were often unhappy. The story of two of these children is told in Kit Pearson's trilogy *The Guests of War.*

women, as was the case everywhere—stopped making stoves and washing machines and refrigerators, and turned out 100,000 machine guns in their place. And unknown to anyone until after the war, inside the massive towers and tunnels of Casa Loma skilful men and women made secret anti-submarine weapons.

People had more and more money in their pockets, but as the war went on, there was less and less to spend it on. You couldn't buy a new car—all the steel was used for tanks and ships and planes and guns. You couldn't buy new tires—they were made from real rubber, and all the real rubber came from countries conquered by Japan, an ally of Germany. If you somehow managed to patch your old tires—on your old car—you couldn't buy gas. Gas was rationed. So were sugar, butter, meat, tea, coffee, honey, syrup, canned fruit, and alcohol. Everybody got a

ration book once a month, with different-coloured coupons that the grocer tore out when you shopped. When you ran out of coupons, you had to wait for next month's book. Sometimes eggs were hard to get, sometimes potatoes. A can of salmon was a rare catch, and often you had to scour the town to find some soap. The new nylon stockings were five dollars a pair—if you bribed a clerk to save some for you. Cuffs vanished from men's pants: the cloth in 54 pairs of them made a uniform. And the kids who built models of Spitfires and Stukas had to give up the hobby: any balsa wood that got through the U-boats in the South Atlantic was used for life jackets, or for filler in real airplanes. Families turned in their old pots and their old cooking fat to be recycled into steel and soap. Children collected six-quart baskets and tinfoil and hangers, and roamed the Toronto ravines harvesting milkweed, used to make fibre and the new synthetic rubber.

Everybody in the city—the "home front"—was part of the war effort. In 1940, when the pilots of the Toronto Squadron flew and fought and died in the skies above London, the Happy Gang changed its theme song to "There'll Always Be an England," whose chorus was:

*There'll always be an England*
*And England shall be free,*

*If England means as much to you*
*As England means to me.*

The same rousing song was played by the Toronto Symphony Orchestra, and sung by everyone in the audience, at the regular Friday afternoon Children's Concerts in Massey Hall. In fact, the song was played so much that even the refugee kids from England got sick of it.

**For other kids** it was a bad time: if their parents or grandparents had come from Germany or Italy or Japan, the countries Canada was fighting, they were called names, and their homes and shops were damaged. Once in a while the children—and their parents—were beaten up. Sometimes the fathers were arrested and put in jail, leaving mothers and children poor and unsupported. In one of the most shameful events of Canada's history, 20,000 Japanese people, many of them born in Canada, had all their property—and all their rights as Canadian citizens—taken from them, by order of Prime Minister King and his government. Then they were penned in prison camps in the British Columbia interior until the war was over. Six-year-old

**A Supermarine Spitfire at City Hall, 1939. The Spitfire was a hotshot acrobatic fighter throughout World War II.**

When the war ended, the celebrations spilled into the streets. Somebody attached streamers to a confused policeman and danced around him as if he were a maypole. Skyrockets, still legal then, whooshed from rooftops all over the city. Soldiers and sailors and airmen kissed all the girls they could find—and the girls kissed them back.

David Suzuki was among them. So were Shizuye Takashima and Joy Kogawa, who tell their stories in *A Child in Prison Camp* and *Naomi's Road*.

Sometimes young people were treated as responsible grown-ups and sometimes as reckless idiots, although this is hardly big news. One law, passed in 1942, kept high schools closed until the end of September so that the students could help with the wheat harvest. Another law, passed by Toronto city council in May 1944, made it a crime for kids under 16 to be on the street after nine o'clock at night—when boys just two years older were dying in Africa and Italy and France.

Seven months after the curfew law the city once again asked young people for help, this time to shovel snow. During the night of December 11, a fierce blizzard swept into southern Ontario. It's still on the record books as the worst winter storm Toronto has ever had. It snowed all that night and all the next day, until it was two feet (0.6 m) deep. The wind lashed it into drifts 15 metres (50 feet) high. A streetcar overturned on Queen; one man died and 43 people were hurt. The Queen Elizabeth Way was closed. You couldn't drive. You could barely walk. One young woman skied to church to marry an airman. Fourteen people died of heart attacks, trying to push through the snow. To obtain milk and bread and coal you had to get to the nearest fire hall, unless you lived near Wellesley and Parliament; there, Acme Farmers Dairy delivered milk by horse and sleigh. At that time Toronto had no snow-clearing machines or ploughs or melters, so the whole town simply stopped. All the schools were closed for two days, and a small army of girls and boys with shovels turned out to help. Strangely, nobody thought to ask how old they were when the clocks struck nine at night.

The last of the snow had barely melted when school was closed once more. It was May 8, 1945, a sunny Tuesday. In most schools the national anthem was just fading away and the teachers were taking attendance. Abruptly, a hundred PA systems stuttered into life, and a hundred principals, their voices perhaps a little shaky, announced that the war in Europe was over.

Kids all over the city poured out of their schools to mingle with the thousands of people in the streets. Downtown, the streetcars clanged their bells, cars honked their horns, churches rang out the good news. Toronto danced; Toronto sang; Toronto cheered; Toronto wept. Toronto did not, however, drink: the powers that be had locked up the liquor stores and bars.

Three months later, when two atomic bombs had annihilated two Japanese cities and 130,000 people (and still counting), the scene was repeated. The Second World War had ended. Of Canada's 16 Victoria Cross winners, 3 called Toronto home. But 3,300 men and women of Toronto would never come home again.

## The Welcome Mat

The soldiers came home. They wanted jobs and houses and cars and babies. And they got them—especially the babies. The decade after the war was known as the baby boom. By 1955, one person in four in Toronto was under 14. Ten years later, one person in three was under 14. Toronto was full of kids.

It was also full of immigrants. In 1920, 8 out of every 10 people in the city were of British origin; by 1960, only 5 out of 10—half—claimed that heritage. In 1961, only 3 out of every 100

people in Toronto were non-white; 40 years later, 54 out of every 100 would be non-white. Thousands and thousands of refugees from all over the world wanted a future free of fear and hunger, a future better than their past. They looked around for a good country to live in—and they picked Canada. They looked around for a good city to live in—and they picked Toronto.

And Toronto put out the welcome mat.

Street hockey, Toronto vs. Montreal

That tidal wave of people changed Toronto forever. No longer was Toronto a white, English, Protestant town. The world had arrived—and, happily for all who live here, Toronto let the world in. There are now 77 different communities and 100 languages in the city, and the city is the richer for it. Toronto has more Italians than Bologna or Florence. It has more blacks than Kingston, Jamaica. And it has more Chinese than any city in the world outside of China.

There have been Quakers in Toronto ever since Timothy Rogers brought a bunch up from Vermont in 1800. For a

**Early telephone booth, when a call cost a nickel**

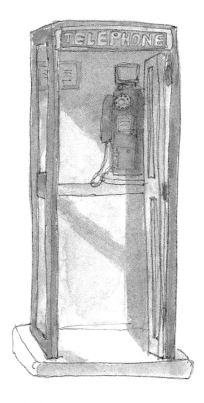

century and a half Toronto has had its Methodists and Baptists. But now there are Buddhists and Baha'is, Christian Scientists and Krishna Consciousness Seekers, Muslims and Moravians, African Episcopalians and Chinese Pentecostalists, Evangelicals and Overcomers and Unitarians, Sikhs and Spiritualists and Swedenborgians. We have half as many Jews as Tel Aviv, and three times as many Catholics as Anglicans.

All of this would give Bishop Strachan a stomach ache. But it gives Toronto colour and class and life, books and plays and paintings and every kind of music—and wonderful restaurants.

## A Big Mother— and a Big Daddy

In 1951 the government counted all the people, including all the new kids and all the new Canadians. In Toronto they numbered 1,200,000, spilling out into the suburbs and beyond. And they all needed houses and roads and parks and schools and sewers and water and electricity and firefighters and cops. It was time to think big. It was time to think Metro.

Metropolitan (the word means "mother-city") Toronto was born April 15, 1953. It was called the most important city experiment on the continent, one that other Canadian and American cities admired and studied and learned from. Its first boss—a kind of super-mayor—was Fred Gardiner, known as "Big Daddy." Fred called the shots. He gathered together in a federation—something like the provinces under Ottawa—the city of Toronto and all the "little cities" that then encircled it: East York, Etobicoke, Forest Hill, Leaside, Long Branch, Mimico, New Toronto, North York, Scarborough, Swansea, Weston, and York.

Later, in a 1967 streamlining, these 13 "cities" became 6: Etobicoke, North York, York, East York, Scarborough, and Toronto. Each of them had its own council, and each sent representatives to the 37-member Metropolitan Toronto Council (12 from Toronto, 25 from the five other cities). Each city sold its own water, collected its own garbage, had its own firefighters, looked after its own side streets and parks and playgrounds, had its own school system and its own dog catcher. Metro looked after everything else—the most important being the main roads and expressways—but also had some say in everything the six cities did.

There were power struggles and arguments, some silly, some serious, and even a brawl or two, but for the next 40 years, for most of its 3.5 million people, for most of its 62,000 hectares (240 square miles), Metro Toronto worked. The mother-city was a success.

## The Tubing of Toronto

The subway helped to make it so, though few believed it would at the time. For five long years Yonge Street was a disaster. For five years it was again the muddy swamp it had been before it had a name—especially after a steam shovel cut a water main and the resulting geyser threw a worker 3 metres (10 feet) into the air.

Finally, on March 3, 1954, one-time mayor Horatio Hocken's 1911 dream came true. The mayor and the premier, neither of whom had swung a pick or driven a pile, managed to pull a switch—and the first subway in Canada began its 7.2-kilometre (4.5-mile) run from Union Station to Eglinton. On its first day in service, 100,000 people took a ride on the subway.

## Boyds Fly Coop

One news item reported over CBLT television on its first day in service, in September 1952, was the breakout of the Boyd Gang from the Don Jail. Edwin Alonzo Boyd, the son of a policeman, didn't follow in his father's footsteps—

Mayor Fred Gardiner was a cigar-chomping, derby-hatted dynamo of a man whose ideas matched his huge bulk. His name lives on in the car-choked Expressway laid down on the old lakeside Native trail.

although his father's footsteps might have followed him. Born in 1914, Ed was a teenager when the Great Depression hit. He left school, became a hobo, and, like so many, had a few problems with the police as he wandered around Canada. Again like so many, he joined the army when World War II began. At its end he couldn't settle down, and he couldn't find a good job either, so in 1949 he went into business for himself—as a bill collector. The bills were tens and twenties and fifties, and he collected them from banks. He robbed six Toronto banks in a year and a half, but seven was his unlucky number: he got caught in October 1951 in a bank at Yonge and Lawrence.

In the Don Jail he teamed up with some fellows who shared his enthusiasm for instant banking, and on November 4 they broke out. The Boyd Gang hit two banks in a month before being recaptured the following March.

Once again the jail couldn't hold them: they escaped on September 8, 1952, the day Toronto TV was born. After the biggest manhunt in Canadian history, they were cornered in a barn at Leslie and Sheppard. Sentenced to life—which in Canada usually means 20 years with time off for good behaviour—Ed Boyd was freed after 14 years. He changed his name, moved out west—and later collected a stack of bills as consultant to a movie about his life.

## The Big Swim

It is two years later. A 16-year-old girl travels from her home at 134 Hallam Street in Toronto to Youngstown, New York. There, at seven minutes past 11 p.m. on September 8, 1954, she steps into the cold waters of Lake Ontario not far from the spot where William Berczy, with an American sheriff on his tail, took off for Canada.

**The bus stops here**

William used a barge. Marilyn Bell, a tidy little package of power and perseverance, will swim. Her goal: to be the first person to swim across Lake Ontario, a distance of 52 kilometres (32 miles). All that night she swims, the water numbing her flesh, the lampreys sucking at her legs and back, the oil slicks making her sick; but still she swims and swims. The sun comes up and half blinds her, but still she swims, robot-like, knowing only that she must reach the shore. To that shore, as the news spreads, come the people of Toronto. At first there are a hundred, two hundred, then a thousand. At noon there are tens of thousands, and at dusk, hundreds of thousands. Everybody in Toronto—and, by radio, everybody in Canada—waits for the little teenager.

Marilyn slips in and out of consciousness. She's so tired that every breath is an ordeal. But still she swims. She will have no memory of touching the slime-covered breakwater 20 hours and 59 minutes after she entered the water, no recollection of the horns and whistles and cheers that echo through the city. She is the talk of the town, the girl of the hour, a true Canadian heroine. She's showered with money and flooded with movie and TV offers. Marilyn smiles—and quietly goes back to school.

Later, she will swim the English

In 1954, Hurricane Hazel roared into Toronto and dumped a Niagara of rain on ground already soaked by autumn storms. Altogether, more than 100 billion litres (22 billion gallons) of water fell on Greater Toronto. Holland Marsh became an instant lake, on which farmhouses bobbed like cardboard boxes. The Humber, the Don, Highland and Etobicoke creeks, every stream and brook and rivulet rose, swelled, and burst. Avalanches of churning water rushed towards the lake.

Channel and the Juan de Fuca Strait on the west coast, the youngest person to do so. And three years after her Lake Ontario triumph, in 1957, she will quietly marry a boy named Joe.

## The Big Blow

Across the same lake, five weeks later, came another powerful female. Her name was Hurricane Hazel, and she moved a lot faster than Marilyn. What's more, she was a killer. She'd already made a mess of Haiti and the U.S. east coast. The body count so far was 139. Then she moved inland at 120 k.p.h. (75 m.p.h.) and the Toronto weather office issued a heavy rain warning. Everybody yawned and went to bed. Halfway across the lake, Hazel collided with a huge mass of cold air going the other way. This stirred her up something fierce.

In Toronto, hundreds of trees were ripped out by the roots and fell into the flooded rivers. Forty bridges were swept away. Half a block of Raymore Drive in Etobicoke disappeared, with 36 people still asleep in their beds and others screaming from rooftops. Cars, trucks, trailers, backyard swings, garages, telephone poles, tricycles, tumbled end over end in the torrent. Streets too near the rivers—where they should not have been allowed in the first place—collapsed and vanished. Houses too near the rivers— where they should not have been allowed—toppled and broke apart. Five volunteer firemen from the Kingsway Lambton Department drowned, their fire engine swept from under them. Another fireman was handed a four-month-old baby named Nancy by the Thorpe family, who chose to wait out the flood in their house. They drowned, and Nancy was an orphan. And after sailing down the Etobicoke Creek in an empty house, and after twice chewing through the ropes that tied her at an emergency shelter, a dog named Lassie found her way back to the old couple who loved her.

**The morning after Hazel**

The next morning it was sunny, with only a light breeze. A stunned Toronto counted its losses: $25,000,000 in property damage, 4,000 people homeless—and 81 dead. It was the worst disaster the city had ever suffered.

On September 8, 1952, at 7:15 p.m., CBLT, Canada's first English-language TV channel, sent out its signal—with its logo upside down. Featured that night were the news, the weather, and a brilliant 21-year-old pianist named Glenn Gould—and then the news again. It was all in black-and-white, and viewed—by the few who owned a set—on a round seven-inch (18 cm) screen that looked like a porthole and cost $300. Everyone agreed it was a miracle.

Out of the tragedy, however, came good: 13 dams were built, flood control became a reality, and the land along the rivers would never again be used for houses, but for parks and recreation. If you look for the Humber River on a map, you'll see, on both sides, a wide emerald border. After she took so much on that terrible night, Hazel left a gift.

## The Trashing of Toronto

If William Lyon Mackenzie had dropped in around mid-century, he might have put something else on the coat of arms: a bulldozer.

Between 1955 and 1965, 10,000 buildings were torn down. Between 1965 and 1975, another 18,000 vanished. Even people who lived in Toronto sometimes lost their bearings. Leave town for a week and you came back a stranger.

# 1954 to 1990

## Bulldozers, BMWs, and Bag Ladies

The neighbourhood is no longer as lively; the action has shifted west and north. Some of our best old buildings, including the Stock Exchange, have been destroyed. The entire block west of the Flatiron Building will soon be flattened for a parking lot. (This was called "urban renewal.") The city now has more tools to fight winter: note the snowplough on Front Street.

**In** an orgy of destruction verging on the berserk, the big property owners— soon called "developers," although sometimes it's hard to see what they develop except their bank accounts— with the politicians cheering them on, levelled half the city, just the way their forebears had hacked down all the trees as soon as they stepped ashore.

It didn't matter that those buildings were our history. Down they came: the Mechanics' Institute; Egerton Ryerson's Normal School; John Howard's Insane Asylum at 999 Queen West; the Armoury, where so many Toronto boys had lined up to die; the glitzy Dufferin Gate of the Ex; the Yonge Street Arcade, built in 1884 at Adelaide, and, with 25 shops under one roof, a kind of early mall; most of Toronto Street; Timothy Eaton's house on Lowther; and the Sunnyside Pavilion—bought as scrap by a junk dealer for $335.

And what did we get instead?

**We got office buildings**—2 million square metres (21 million square feet) of them by 1965, mostly along the subway line, and mostly ugly. (This was just the start: by 1990, Metro had more than

**Developers saving face: modern skyscrapers are built on top of architecture from our past.**

11.6 million square metres/125 million square feet of offices, not counting the little buildings or those over stores.)

We got apartments. In 1950 a third of the city's dwellings were apartments; in the 1960s the proportion rose to half. We got a new word too: *high-rise*.

We got parking lots. And parking lots. And parking lots. Lots and lots and lots of lots. But never enough, and cars spilled into the streets. Drivers fought for parking spots like dogs for a bone. And after September 14, 1958, they had something else to worry about: the first pedestrian crosswalk was painted on the pavement.

We got shopping centres. Sunnybrook, in 1952, was the first, at the corner of Bayview and Eglinton, with 17 stores jammed into an L. Don Mills was next, for all the people in Canada's "model suburb" (built by millionaire E.P. Taylor, who said that nobody could have a blue roof). By 1966 there were 227 shopping centres all around the town. At last you could hang out at a mall. The one that everybody talked about, though, was Yorkdale, sprawled along the edge of the new superhighway. At the time, its 100 stores and 6,500 parking spaces made it the biggest shopping centre in Canada. (West Edmonton Mall, with 800 stores and a full-scale amusement park, described by writer Bill Kinsella as "ten acres of plastic ... jewellery and french fries," was far in the future.)

We got bars—even though we called them cocktail lounges at first. Toronto voted to go "wet" in 1947 (except for West Toronto, which stayed thirsty until 1998) and before you could hiccup, the Silver Rail was built at Yonge and Shuter. Soon there were nearly as many taverns per person as there were in 1800.

**But by far** the most spectacular thing we got was the new City Hall. If we don't count the little town hall of 1831, destroyed by the 1849 fire, this is Toronto's third city hall—and all three are still standing. Only the council chamber—now an art gallery in the St. Lawrence Market—is left of the first one. But all of Edward Lennox's lovely old pile of granite remains, even though it's been converted into a nest of courts that process petty criminals like pigs in a packing house. And right across the street is the new, new, new City Hall.

Toronto's rules about drinking alcoholic beverages used to be strange and complicated. In some places you had to eat if you wanted to drink; in some you weren't allowed to eat if you drank; in some only men could drink; and in others men could drink only if they brought women. It was a puzzle.

1954 to 1990

Had it not been for Toronto's first non-Anglo-Saxon, non-Protestant mayor, Nathan Phillips, the City Hall wouldn't be there. Nathan, a lawyer born in Brockville in 1892, and a Toronto alderman for 27 years, was "Mayor of All the People," as he proudly said, from 1955 to 1962. And he wanted a new office. He ran a contest and got 520 entries from architects in 44 countries. The winner was Viljo Revell of Finland—and his design was a shocker to many a straitlaced Torontonian. Big Daddy Gardiner called it the Taj Mahal—and he wasn't being nice. Somebody else called it a "streamlined privy, with two curved walls shielding the [toilet] seat in the centre."

Nate got his way. With its triumphant design, its huge public square—with space for a rink, rock concerts, receptions, and the revels and occasional riots of New Year's Eve—City Hall, known all over the world, is a place Toronto people are proud of and tourists take pictures of. Now if it only had a few more trees ...

**In the pink at City Hall rink**

And on May 17, 1969, at 3777 Keele Street, a much smaller building opened. It had two golden arches. It served hamburgers. McFood—the counter culture—had arrived.

## Hair, Hash, and Hippies

Old buildings aren't the only things under attack in the sixties. These are the years of youth power, as the baby-boom kids turn into teenagers; and of youth protest—against war, against racism, against sexism, against injustice, against their puzzled parents, and often, it seems, against soap, combs, and clean underwear. Long hair is in, lipstick is out. Ties are out, tie-dyes are in. It's a time of beards, beads, body paint, bare feet, and being different; a time to goof

In the 1960s, half the kids in Toronto ended up in Yorkville, for a day, a week, a month, a year. They were called hippies, or heads, or flower children, or "deliberate hobos," but many bore the names of the "first families" of Toronto, of the wealthy and powerful.

Rochdale College became known as "the 18-storey high" and "the largest drugstore in North America"—and we're not talking chewable vitamins and hair gel. Rochdale was born in hope but killed by dope, like some of the kids who lived there. It's now a senior citizens' home.

off, drop out, smoke up, and turn on.

And the place to do all that is Yorkville—the Yorkville where a later generation can buy a $200 ballpoint pen, and where the price of a teddy bear will pay the rent.

Some come to crash with half a

The well-travelled passport of Glen Gould, Canada's most brilliant classical pianist, who debuted with the Toronto Symphony Orchestra at age 14. When he was 22, he recorded Bach's *Goldberg Variations* to enormous international acclaim. A strange fellow, Gould often wore an overcoat, gloves, and a scarf indoors and in midsummer.

dozen others in a room or two above a coffee house; some to cruise the streets, looking and being looked at. Some come to beg, or steal, or starve, or deal; and some of those will find refuge in Digger House, founded in 1967 by June Callwood—who will be jailed the next year for trying to help some broken, frightened kids. The charge: "creating a disturbance."

**And everywhere** there is music. In one coffee house, called the Mynah Bird, is Neil Young; in another the voices of Ian and Sylvia Tyson blend in a folk song. This kind of music doesn't scare the grown-ups too much.

But screaming from a curbside tape deck is something called the Rolling Stones, and they are screaming "I Can't Get No Satisfaction." *This* scares the grown-ups. A lot.

These are the grown-ups who swayed to the 1950s hits "Why Do Fools Fall in Love?" by the Diamonds, four nice boys who once sang in St. Thomas Aquinas Church on Glenholme Avenue; or "Sh-Boom," top of the charts in 1954, by the Crew Cuts, a short-haired quartet out of the St. Michael's Boys' Choir. Mothers forget they wept and fainted when Frank Sinatra sang "I'll Never Smile Again"—written by Torontonian Ruth Lowe, who smiled a lot as the royalty cheques came in. And fathers forget they once won trophies for doing the Dirty Boogie.

Rock 'n' roll freaks them out. Bill Haley's bad enough, when he and his Comets rock around the clock at Maple Leaf Gardens in 1956. Worse still is Elvis (The Pelvis) Presley in a skin-tight gold suit, singing "Love Me Tender" and "Let Me Be Your Teddy Bear" to 20,000 frenzied kids. And then the Beatles arrive in 1964, and teenagers pay the enormous sum of $5.50 to scream all the way through "I Want to Hold Your Hand" and "She Loves You." Yeah. Yeah. Yeah.

Some of those kids go on to attend Rochdale College, an experimental, student-run free school on Bloor across from the Medical Arts Building (which turns out to be handy—see sidebar).

Some of them go back to their homes in Moore Park and Rosedale and Forest Hill, cut their hair, put on their shoes, and get jobs.

And some go into politics.

## The Reformers

In the early seventies, aghast at what was happening to their city, several young men—John Sewell, Karl Jaffary, and David Crombie, together with the not quite so young William Kilbourn, whose ancestors had seen the little town of York the same year as William Berczy— were elected to city council.

The Toronto Reference Library, with its glass elevator shaft and its 45 kilometres (28 miles) of shelves, was designed by Raymond Moriyama—who, like Joy Kogawa and David Suzuki, spent part of his childhood in an internment camp as a "dangerous alien."

Their creed was straightforward: don't wreck, restore; don't pave, plant; don't make a parking lot, make a park. They pushed for subways and streetcars over the stench of exhaust, for ravines instead of roads, for homes rather than high-rises. Throughout the seventies the Force was with them, with first David and then John serving as mayor. The bulldozers were stopped in their tracks.

The Spadina Expressway, planned as a north-south slash through the city's heart, was stopped at Eglinton; the old railway tracks and abandoned warehouses along the waterfront were partly replaced with parks, theatres, shops, and housing; and much of the insane destruction of older properties halted.

Holy Trinity Church, built in 1843, was saved, and the Eaton Centre went up around it. The house of Enoch Turner, the generous brewer, was saved. Union Station, that fine old temple of fume, was saved. The home of William Campbell—the judge who awarded damages to Lyon Mackenzie back in

**Judge Campbell's house on the move**

1826—was saved, and in a six-hour operation that half the city watched, its 300 tons were trundled from Adelaide and Frederick to University and Queen.

The buildings that rose were for *all* the people, not just a few developers: Ontario Place, with its children's playground, its Cinesphere with the giant curved screen that puts you right in the picture, and its Forum (now the Molson Amphitheatre) for performing artists, with room for 8,000 (now 16,000) people; the Ontario Science Centre, full of "hands-on" exhibits, and the Toronto Zoo, both world-famous; and the Toronto Reference Library at Asquith and Yonge. (One of the stores torn down

to make way for the library was Parker's Cleaners, founded by that same R. Parker who'd run into the curb in 1899.) Yet while the bulldozers were temporarily stalled, and the developers sulking and stymied, three structures arose that were portents of the eighties, symbols of the modern city, what some have called twentieth-century cathedrals.

**In 1977** the old Eaton's store at Queen and Yonge closed its doors. Five days later the Eaton Centre opened. Timothy, whose huge bronze statue brooded at the door until 1999, would have been pleased. Designed by Eberhard Zeidler, a young architect—Ontario Place is another of his creations—who was in the post-war wave of European immigrants, the Eaton Centre was a mega-mall of glass and steel and plants. It stretched from Dundas to Richmond, with Eaton's on one end, Simpson's on the other, and 330 stores in between, all ready to take your money. And there's always been plenty for the taking: more tourists visit the Eaton Centre than any other place in Canada.

A month later the Royal Bank Plaza thrust itself skyward at Front and Bay. It was on the right corner: 150 years before, it had been the site of Holland House, a mansion owned by one of the Boultons, the richest family in Upper Canada. With such a heritage it was no surprise that 70,000 grams of gold coated the windows. It was also in the right neighbourhood: around it rose the Scotia Tower, the three (later four) ebony towers of the TD Centre, the silvery cliff of Commerce Court, and the 72-storey First Canadian Place, the tallest building in Canada and the tallest bank (with the tallest advertisement—look for the blue "B/M" logo) in the world.

## The Tower

Just as Big Ben says London and the Empire State Building says New York, the third structure built at this time has become Toronto's trademark. You can see it from Buffalo, you can see it from Barrie, you can see it from anywhere in Toronto. In fact, it's hard not to see it. It's the CN Communications Tower—the Tower of Babble—built to make the sights and sounds sent by radio, telephone, and television easier and clearer to see and hear, and to make them travel farther.

The Tower is tall. In fact, it's the tallest free-standing structure on earth. To be precise, it's 553 metres (1,815 feet) tall, which is five and a half football fields stacked up end to end. It cost $57 million, which works out to $1,030.13 per centimetre, and it took 1,537 workers 40 months to build it. One of those workers, "Sweet William" Eustace, parachuted from the top a few months before the official opening. He landed on the Gardiner Expressway, got

**Meals on wheels? Refreshments at the ROM.**

In 1891, the de-naming of the wards occurred. Gone were St. Andrew's Ward, St. Patrick's Ward, St. George's, St. James', and St. David's wards, together with half a dozen others. In their stead were Ward 1, Ward 2, Ward 3, etc. Toronto lost some of its British saintliness, which was probably a good thing; but it also lost some of its personality, which was too bad.

arrested, got fired, and got famous—all in less than a minute. Three years later, Toronto high school student Patrick Bailie dropped an egg from the 342-metre (1,122-foot) mark. The egg didn't break—but the egg-dropping record (189 metres/620 feet) did.

The Tower has the highest revolving restaurant, nightclub, and observation deck in the world; enough concrete in it to make a walkway to Kingston; and 2 million visitors a year. The elevator takes 58 seconds to go from bottom to top—or vice versa. This is good to know if you're at the top in a hurricane, because you might get seasick: the Tower sways 18 inches, about 45 centimetres, from its centre. Not to worry, though: built to withstand 418 k.p.h. (260 m.p.h.) winds—those of the worst tornadoes—and with armour-plated windows and 42 lightning rods to look after the 200 strikes a year, the Tower has a perfect safety record.

## The Eighties

In 1980, Toronto streetcars were stripped of their names and given numbers instead. It was the latest invasion of the number crunchers, which had begun with house numbering just after Toronto became Toronto. Houses on the north and west sides of streets were to use even numbers, those on the south and east odd numbers, with Yonge Street the big east/west divide.

The names of houses and grand estates became the names of streets, and as the owners of those estates sold their land, the dwellings built on it took numbers. Thus we have Homewood, Spadina, Rosedale, Davenport, Grange. Berkeley was once Berkeley House, owned by the trigger-happy John Small; Dovercourt was once Dover Court, where Richard Denison hung his hat; Runnymede Road takes its name from John Scarlett's 1838 house on Dundas Street; Grand Opera Lane recalls the magnificent Victorian showplace; and if you listen hard, you may still hear the slap of a beaver's tail or the snap of an alligator's jaw on Piper Street.

The telephone exchanges were next on the hit list. For 60 years the Toronto exchanges had had names—easy-to-remember, melodious, historic, neighbourly names like MOhawk, HUdson, RUssell, HOward, ELgin, WAverley,

ADelaide, MIdway, ORchard. To call Eaton's you dialled AD 5011. To put an ad in the *Star* you phoned WA 3636. To sell your house you called A.E. LePage at EL 1464. But in 1960 all these old friends were disconnected, and Toronto had to dial seven numbers instead—the first Canadian city to do so. Too bad.

And then the streetcars. No longer can you board a Queen car; you squeeze onto a 501. You don't wait for a St. Clair streetcar; you look down the line for a 512. The 200-year-old name Dundas, alive with story and alight with memory, is now 505—which somehow fails to stir the blood.

**In a way,** this itch to play the numbers game was the mark—or perhaps the scar—of the 1980s. Things are numbered only when there are more and

In the 1980s a place to live was so scarce and so expensive that, for the first time in Toronto's history, an ordinary family couldn't hope to buy a home. A house bought for $75,000 in 1980 sold for $300,000 ten years later. The bachelor apartment in its basement (when it was vacant, which was just about never) rented for $750 a month. By 1990 it cost more to live in Toronto than anywhere else in North America.

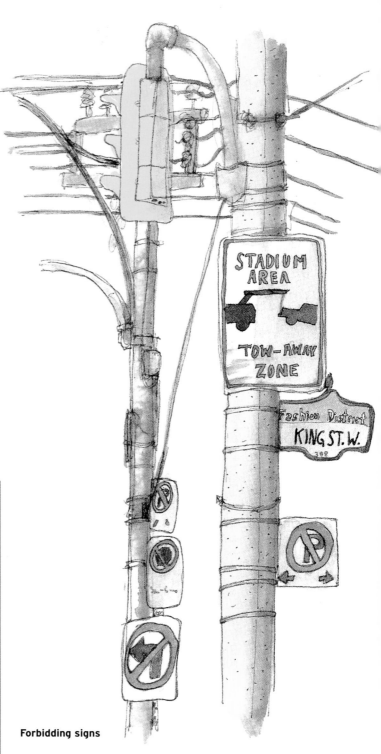

**Forbidding signs**

more of them to keep track of. And if there's one word that fit the decade, it was the four-letter word MORE.

The main thing the city got more of was people: 65,000 of them—the population of Dartmouth or Kamloops—moved to Greater Toronto every year. More people meant more of everything

**The bag lady and the BMW: poverty and wealth in downtown Toronto**

else: more cars, from Jags to Jettas, from Blazers to BMWs, from Micras to Maseratis; more crime, from shoplifting to swarming, from mugging to murder; more crowds, in supermarkets and streetcars, in parking lots and picnic spots. You even had to line up to get more money from the "instant" bank machines.

**But more people** also meant more plays in more theatres, like the Young People's Theatre (renamed the Lorraine Kimsa Theatre for Young People in 2001); more books, and more bookstores to sell them, including the world's biggest children's bookstore; more music, more kinds of music, and more young musicians, like the Toronto Boys' Choir and the Toronto Youth Orchestra, not to mention the Nylons, Martha and the Muffins, Sharon, Lois and Bram, and Raffi; and more art on more walls—including the outside wall of the Gooderham Building.

Some people did more, and we know their names:
› swimmer Vicki Keith, who doggedly crossed all five of the Great Lakes, the first person ever to do so
› biologist Lap-Chee Tsui, who just as doggedly peered at 100,000 genes at Sick Kids Hospital, until in 1989 he found the one that carries cystic

fibrosis, bringing hope to parents and children all over the world

> Pauline McGibbon, first woman to be just about everything, including Chancellor of the University of Toronto, Governor of Upper Canada College, Life Member of the Chamber of Commerce, and Lieutenant-Governor of Ontario
> sprinter Ben Johnson, who ran 100 metres, won a medal, had a drug test, lost a medal, and became the only man in history to go from hero to zero in 9.79 seconds
> journalist June Callwood, who founded Casey House, a hospice and home for those dying from AIDS—and later got fired from the *Globe and Mail* for being too "humanitarian"
> Garth Drabinsky, a high-flying movie mogul and impresario, who matched 1,500 samples of old paint and gave back to Toronto the landmark Pantages Theatre of 1920. Seventy years after they first saw it as a silent movie, the people of Toronto lined up again to see *The Phantom of the Opera*—as a musical this time.
> ballet dancer Veronica Tennant, a Bishop Strachan "old girl," who got two honorary degrees from universities, won the Toronto Arts Award, and wrote a children's book called *The Nutcracker*

> first baseman Freddy McGriff, whose 36 home runs in 1989 helped the Blue Jays win the American League East pennant

But nobody knew the names of the 25,000 homeless people who wandered through the city, layered in clothing and laden with plastic bags, who cadged meals at hostels and caught naps in cardboard boxes.

## Home of the Dome

Everybody had a name for Toronto's new playground, SkyDome. The Dome is home to the Blue Jays and the Argonauts, but it's also seen track meets, dirt bike races, operas, and rock concerts. It

*The Audience*, by Michael Snow, on the outside wall of SkyDome

**Blue recycling boxes of the 1990s in front of Victorian houses of the 1890s**

squats beside the CN Tower, a couple of blocks from where the ammunition dump blew up in 1813. A young teacher in Wallaceburg, Kellie Watson, gave it its name, in a contest that drew close to 13,000 suggestions. Her prize? Two tickets to every SkyDome show for the rest of her life.

The workers started digging in October 1986. They moved 300,000 cubic metres (400,000 cubic yards) of earth, and found a pocket spyglass, a cannon from the War of 1812, the gold handle of a cane, a century-old mustard jar, and 1,822 bottles. They also poured enough cement to make a sidewalk from Toronto to Montreal, plugged in the JumboTron, at 330 square metres (3,500 square feet) the biggest TV set ever, and

put in 1,280 toilets. And when all the Dome's switches were on, it burned enough electricity to light 25,000 homes. SkyDome was supposed to cost $125 million. It didn't. It cost more than $500 million.

As if that weren't enough—or even too much—there was also an 11-storey, 350-room hotel in the place, a health

SkyDome was the world's first domed stadium with a retractable roof, which means it pulls in and pushes out like a telescope, or a pussycat's claws. The roof weighs 10,000 tons, give or take a ton or two—about the weight of 200 large dinosaurs—and takes 20 minutes to open or close.

The Arrow, designed and built by Toronto's A.V. Roe Company in the 1950s, was a state-of-the-art interceptor jet. In a move that angered many, when the Canadian government cancelled its contract for the planes, all the plans were shredded and all the planes destroyed.

club whose fees would sicken your bank account, box seats that rented for $225,000 a year, an electronic playground known as Skyplace crammed with video games, and a restaurant where hot dogs cost $6.50. Some people were going to make a lot of money from the Dome—but the taxpayers of Toronto wouldn't be among them.

On opening night, June 4, 1989, the Dome generated more big numbers: 30,000 balloons rose in a cloud of colour, and 780 dancers—the longest chorus line in history—kicked up a storm. Really. It started to rain. They closed the roof. It went on raining. The $40-million state-of-the-art roof—the most expensive umbrella in the world—had sprung a leak.

## The Jewel by the Water

If we could magically transport the Simcoe family forward in time, from that morning in July 1793 to one 200 years later, young Sophia would stand open-mouthed once again. What would she see this time? Not red pines 20 storeys high; there are few trees left near the harbour. Not the Queen's Rangers swinging axes; only their ghosts remain at Fort York.

**CHAPTER EIGHT**

**1990 to 2002+**

**Towards the Millennium ... and Beyond**

And this is how that wilderness of five centuries ago looks today. The Gooderham Building is dwarfed by towers of glass, concrete, and steel. Look at what replaced the old stone Bank of Toronto on the corner of Wellington and Church. Trees are back in style as the city tries to conceal the scars of the fifties and sixties. Overhead wires have gone underground. The parking lot is now a park named for Little Albert. Beside the Flatiron Building a movie is being shot— a common sight in "Hollywood North." On the corner, right behind Molly, the family dog, stands Johnny Wales; and in a black track suit, just about to cross the street, is Claire Mackay.

**These** days, Sophia would see kids, hundreds of them, doing amazing stuff. She'd see Harbourfront in the summer, a children's paradise, where she could learn:

> ballet, painting, moviemaking, photography, sculpture, and theatre;
> tennis, golf, soccer, sailing, canoeing, and kayaking;
> chess, Dungeons and Dragons, and magic;
> juggling, clowning, and the flying trapeze.

She could even learn how to build a clock that runs on lemon juice.

**The docklands** at the city's foot had long lain ramshackle and idle when, in 1974, a few truckloads of government money and a few dozen determined people set out to transform it into "Harbourfront," a place where Torontonians would want to hang out. It started small, with music and poetry readings and plays, but it grew up quickly. Now it's a 4-hectare (10-acre) non-profit arts and entertainment centre, visited by 3 million people each year—who all get in for free. With more than 450 community groups sharing in the fun, the place is jumping year-round—a lively reincarnation for the harbour that first drew humans to Toronto.

## Harbourfront and Harry Potter

The Reading Series at Harbourfront has been going on for more than a quarter of a century. It runs all year, but its crowning event is the 11-day International Festival of Authors (IFOA) in October. It's the best in the world. More than 2,500 authors from every corner of the globe have read to Toronto. For most of its years the Festival only rarely invited a children's author, but then, brilliant as a comet, came *Harry Potter and the Philosopher's Stone*. The world took notice, and so did Toronto. J.K. Rowling got an invitation to the IFOA.

**On October 24, 2000,** more than 20,000 children, most of them dressed as wizards—with pointy hats and telltale lightning bolts on their foreheads—flocked to SkyDome, with bewildered teachers, parents, and grandparents trailing behind. The Dome was decked out like a big black tent. There were fireworks, and magicians, and balloons, and weird announcements: "The 423rd Quidditch World Cup has been cancelled. There are too many Muggles in the audience."

For openers, two Canadian authors did their stuff. Ken Oppel read from *Silverwing*, the first book in his bat fantasy trilogy, and Tim Wynne-Jones read

## The Mayors and the Megacity

A very different woman made a big splash in Toronto nine years before J.K. Rowling. In 1991, Toronto woke up to discover it had a new mayor, who would henceforth be addressed as HER Worship. For the first time in Toronto's 160-year history, its citizens had chosen a woman to lead them. Mayor June Rowlands presided over two notable events: (1) She made the decision to construct a new subway line, Sheppard East, from Yonge Street to Don Mills. (2) She made a Canadian rock band famous.

The Barenaked Ladies were scheduled to play at Nathan Phillips Square on New Year's Eve, but Mayor June suddenly said, "No way!" She thought their name was "offensive," that it turned women into "objects." The story made all the North American papers, with a photo of the band on every front page. Shortly thereafter the Barenaked Ladies signed a huge record deal, and soon they were international stars.

Mayor June, Toronto's first female mayor, was followed by Mayor Barbara, its second. Barbara Hall, a quiet community worker, teacher, and lawyer, worked hard to revive the spirit of reform initiated by David Crombie, William Kilbourn, and John Sewell in the 1970s. She restored some order—and courtesy—to

**The Toronto Island ferry takes you from traffic to tranquillity in 15 minutes.**

from his mystery *The Boy in the Burning House*. Then the lights were dimmed, a single spotlight came on, and into its glow stepped the small blonde woman every child had come to see, to hear, and just to be near—Joanna K. Rowling.

She read from chapter four of Book Four, *Harry Potter and the Goblet of Fire*. As one reporter later wrote, "You could have heard a wand drop." Until, of course, the minutes-long rolling thunder of applause when she stopped. It was the biggest single reading in the history of the world.

**1990 to 2002+**

the often chaotic and rude council meetings, and did her best to unite the many segments of multicultural Toronto. Her best, however, wasn't quite good enough, and in the election of 1997 the city chose Mel Lastman, who'd been mayor of North York for 25 years, as its main man.

Mel, Toronto's colourful 62nd mayor, is a lot like its first, William Lyon Mackenzie. For one thing, he's short. For another, most of the hair on his head wasn't there to start with. For a third thing, he's a noisy fellow, not at all shy about letting you know how he feels. And for a final thing, he often forgets to think before he speaks or acts—which lands him in deep trouble from time to time. One journalist described him as "a rough-and-tumble guy, the son of immigrants, a brash, self-made millionaire ... [who] represents the new ethnic Toronto ..." There is a lot of the irrepressible and rambunctious boy in him, and ordinary folk are fond of him for that—fond enough to return him to the mayor's office in 2000 for a second term.

During the Lastman regime, Toronto underwent two massive and dramatic structural changes, both ordered by the

The prize-winning six-storey Galleria, a climate-controlled arcade of glass and light, forms the "spine" of BCE Place, an office/retail complex covering a city block in downtown Toronto.

**Fugitive from the animal patrol**

provincial government. The first was dryly called Local Services Realignment, nicknamed "downloading." Here's how it was supposed to work: the province would put up all the money for education, and in return the city would pay for just about everything else—water, sewers, public transportation, low-cost housing, libraries, parks, pools, rinks, dental care for needy old people, breakfast programs for hungry children ... and on and on, to the end of a very long list. The province said it would be an even swap; it wasn't. The city soon found itself dangerously in debt, to the tune of $300 million a year by 2001, and was forced to cut or abolish many of those services that had made Toronto a safe and clean and caring place to live.

Toronto the Good wasn't nearly so good any more.

The second big change was "amalgamation." On January 1, 1998, the old Metro structure, in place since 1953, vanished. Its six distinct municipalities (Etobicoke, North York, York, East York, Scarborough, and Toronto), each with considerable power over its own affairs, were combined into one mega-city, whose name was Toronto. Henceforth there would be one fire department, one police force, one library system, one public school board, one separate school board, one parks department, one division of garbage collectors, one set of dog catchers.

It didn't happen smoothly or overnight. In fact, it's still happening. There were thousands of glitches, tens of thousands of grumbles. There were long delays and short tempers. There were mix-ups about money, about who would pay for what. Many people felt they'd lose their sense of belonging, their ties to a particular pocket of land, their roots. But slowly, sometimes creakily, often reluctantly, the new jumbo-sized Toronto is starting to work. And in their hearts people continue to cling, perhaps even more fiercely, to their home ground. You can still hear them say with pride, "I grew up in East York" or "I live in Etobicoke." And many, mindful of history,

1990 to 2002+

Maple Leaf Gardens, the "Grand Old Lady of Carlton Street," the "Ice Palace," the "Carlton Street Cashbox," closed for good on February 12, 1999—and a piece of Toronto history closed with it. For 68 years the Leafs had played there; it had been the site of celebration and dejection, of memories and dreams. For 68 years it had seen great champions and great championships, gritty heroism and brilliant goaltending, flashy skating and thrill-a-minute contests. The Leafs now play at the Air Canada Centre on Front Street ("The Hangar"), where new memories and new dreams are being forged.

use even older names, saying, "I'm from Weston (or the Beach or Riverdale or the Junction)." The spirit of neighbourhood, the close and affectionate links of community, live and thrive.

**The Lillian H. Smith branch of Toronto Public Library, at College and Huron streets, is home to one of the best collections of early children's books.**

# Major League Living

All through the 1990s, Toronto was wild about sports. And why not? It had every right to be. With five professional teams —hockey, baseball, football, lacrosse, and (at last!) basketball—and all of them hot to win, the place was Jock Heaven.

### Hockey

Harold Ballard, who had owned the Toronto Maple Leafs since 1971, died in 1990. Few mourned. Ballard was a slightly crazed skinflint who made Scrooge look like Santa Claus. He refused to spend money on the team, and he traded away all the best players. He also fired coaches on a whim. Once, he fired Roger Neilson only to hire him back in desperation. True to his eccentric nature, he ordered Roger to stand behind the bench wearing a garbage bag over his head. (Roger said no.) Ballard became more of a public spectacle when he went to jail for not paying his taxes. The team, and its loyal but heartsore fans, were demoralized during the Ballard years.

So, when millionaire grocer Steve Stavro bought the team in 1991, there was jubilation in Hogtown. Stavro hired Cliff Fletcher as general manager and fiery Pat Burns as coach—and things started to look up. With stars like the beloved Saskatchewan farm kid Wendel Clark ("Captain Crunch"), the cunning and wiry Doug Gilmour, and the powerful Swede Mats Sundin, the Leafs started to win, repeatedly making it into the playoffs.

### Football
In November 1991, the Toronto Argonauts, the city's century-old football club, won the championship Grey Cup game for only the second time in 40 years, beating the Calgary Stampeders 36–21. And then, in 1996 and 1997, they did it again,

against the Edmonton Eskimos and the Saskatchewan Roughriders. The Arab-American Doug Flutie, at 175 centimetres (5'9") not the biggest quarterback in the known world, guided them to victory.

### Baseball
In October 1992, the Toronto Blue Jays won the World Series in six games against the Atlanta Braves, the final game a nail-biter right to the end of the 11th inning. In the bottom of the 11th, with the Jays

**All-star goalie Curtis Joseph – Cujo – played four brilliant seasons with the Maple Leafs**

1990 to 2002

On the night of August 27, 1990, the Blue Jays and the Milwaukee Brewers were all set to play ball when huge clouds of gnats descended through the open roof. The air was so thick with them that the players—not to mention the umpires—couldn't see. Pitcher David Wells put on a beekeeper's mask. It didn't help. The roof was closed, the gnats gradually disappeared, and finally, after 35 minutes, the game began. It was the first "bug delay" in baseball history.

leading 4–3, two Braves were out, but they had a runner on third base. Then speedy Otis Nixon stepped to the plate—and made a bad decision. He bunted. Jays pitcher Mike Timlin scooped it up and lobbed it over to Joe Carter on first base. Otis was out. The Braves lost. And Joe leapt skyward in wild delight. So did all of Toronto.

Then, in October 1993, the Blue Jays did it again! They prevailed over the Philadelphia Phillies in six games, the last one played at SkyDome, with a million Torontonians—and 10 million Canadians—holding their breath at every pitch. Trailing 6–5 in the bottom of the ninth, with two runners on base, Joe Carter moved into the batting box. After two balls and two strikes from Phillies hurler Mitch ("Wild Thing") Williams,

Joe saw a pitch he liked. He swung. He connected. He launched a home run over the left-field fence.

The Blue Jays won, 8–6. And Joe leapt his way around the bases, while long-time Jays broadcaster Tom Cheek shouted, "Touch 'em all, Joe! You'll never hit a bigger home run!" Fans rushed from

SkyDome, the world's first domed stadium ... and a Joe Carter home run.

In 1998 the Film Festival gave birth to Sprockets, a week-long celebration each April of the best films for children, gathered from many countries. Such prizewinners as *Kirikou and the Sorcerers*, *The Monkey's Tale*, and the stunning animation film *Superwhy?* have captivated young audiences. And Sprockets in turn gave birth to Jump Cuts, a mini-festival of videos by kids and for kids.

the Dome and from their homes to hug one another and cheer their way up Yonge Street.

## Basketball

Professional basketball, dead since the Toronto Huskies folded in 1946, returned to the city in May 1994. After years of planning, months of meetings, hundreds of phone calls, and $125 million, the team unveiled its name: the Raptors, chosen after a nationwide contest, and sent in by someone who'd seen the 1993 film *Jurassic Park* too many times. Also revealed were the new team's logo (a dribbling crimson dinosaur with awesome teeth) and its colours (Raptor red, purple, black, and Naismith silver, the last in honour of James Naismith, the Canadian who invented basketball in 1891).

The first tipoff took place on November 3, 1995, at the SkyDome, and more than 33,000 people showed up. Toronto was—and is—totally pumped about hoops.

## Lacrosse

In May 2000, the Toronto Rock, the city's pro lacrosse team, won its second straight league championship, downing the Rochester Knighthawks 14–13 with 1.2 seconds left on the clock. Known as "the fastest game on two feet," lacrosse is an adaptation of the ancient First Nations game of *baggataway*, from an

**Nineteenth-century semi-detached houses, a common downtown style – with different notions of decor**

Ojibwa word for "ball." Popular and widespread long before the Europeans arrived in the New World, lacrosse—not hockey—is Canada's national game and oldest organized sport.

## Tinseltown Toronto

Toronto shares with Vancouver the nickname "Hollywood North." On any given day 25 films are being shot here—on the waterfront, in Kensington Market, at Casa Loma, down in the subway, on the streets of Little Italy, in the shops of Chinatown (north and south), in "Greektown" along the road built 200 years ago by Asa Danforth, on college campuses, east side, west side, all around the town. Sometimes it's hard to get around the huge film vans, the thick cables, the lights, the cameras, the action. During the 1990s, feature-length movies shot in Toronto included *X-Men, Existenz, The Hurricane, Good Will Hunting, The Skulls, Extreme Measures, Short Circuit 2, and Dracula 2000.*

After Los Angeles and New York, Toronto is the third largest film and television centre in the world, helped by an abundance of studios, labs, and highly trained technicians—not to mention the low value of the Canadian dollar. "Hollywood North" means that 40,000 people get jobs and the city gets a whack of money: $1.5 billion a year.

And then there's the Toronto International Film Festival, the second biggest in the world (the one in Cannes, France, is the biggest) and by far the most important in North America. Every September, starting in 1978 but bursting into full bloom in the nineties, Toronto screens upwards of 200 films from around the globe. From around the

**This way to Chinatown**

globe, too, come tens of thousands of tourists, to live it up at the parties, to line up for the movies, and to gawk at the stars who show up to look at themselves. It's a blast.

## Mirvishes and Musicals

When Honest Ed Mirvish bought and refurbished the nearly derelict Royal Alexandra Theatre in 1962, his plan was to restore it to its glory days as a "road-house," a stage for touring shows and plays brought in from elsewhere. And that's exactly what he did, until 1986. In that year his son David—the owner of

In 1948, Ed Mirvish cashed in his wife's $212 insurance policy and opened a store at Bathurst and Bloor. He called it Honest Ed's, and it was the world's first true bargain store. He put up a sign that read, **NAME YOUR OWN PRICE! NO REASONABLE OFFER REFUSED!** You can buy just about anything at Honest Ed's, from twine to wine, wrenches to benches, floor wax to thumbtacks, spaghetti to confetti. Every Christmas, Ed himself gives a turkey to every-body who shows up at the store. Plastered on the windows are cheeky mottoes: "Don't faint at our low prices, there's no place to lie down!" "How cheap can a guy get? Come in and find out!" Honest Ed Mirvish is one of Toronto's favourite people.

what one columnist called "the most elegant private art gallery in Canada" on Markham Street, just around the corner from his dad's bargain department store—founded Mirvish Productions. David wanted to produce and mount his own shows. And that's what he did—with amazing success.

The list of hits is long and lustrous: the classic musicals *Damn Yankees* and *Guys and Dolls*; the Gilbert and Sullivan operettas *The Mikado* and *HMS Pinafore*; *Crazy for You*, starring Mickey Rooney and Toronto's own Barbara Hamilton; the sensational *Les Misérables*, and *Mamma Mia!*, all of which played to sold-out crowds from Buffalo, Detroit, Cleveland, and all parts of Canada month after month after month.

But the Mirvishes weren't finished. In 1993, they built the gorgeous 2,000-seat Princess of Wales Theatre, just a block west of the Royal Alex. The stage, wide and deep, was designed especially for the breathtaking scene in the theatre's first production, *Miss Saigon*, where (just about every day for two years) a helicopter roared in, hovered, and settled on the boards like a giant black bug. *Miss Saigon* was followed by Disney's *Beauty and the Beast*, and in April 2000 Simba and Scar and Nala and Rafiki began to strut their stuff in the spectacular *The Lion King*.

1990 to 2002+

The Pantages Theatre in Toronto (now the Canon) was one of 120 Pantages theatres owned by Pericles Alexander Pantages, a Greek sailor who prospected for gold in the 1890s Yukon gold rush. Things didn't pan out for him, so he opened a saloon instead, featuring vaudeville acts, and made a ton of money. In 1929 he was falsely accused of assaulting a chorus girl. The publicity ruined his reputation and the legal fees ruined his bank account. His name vanished from marquees, and until Garth Drabinsky came along, the Toronto venue was called the Imperial.

Then the Mirvishes added a third showplace. In 1989, Garth Drabinsky had opened the newly restored Pantages Theatre at Dundas and Yonge with the musical *The Phantom of the Opera*. It stayed there for 10 years—the longest-running musical in Toronto history. But Garth went broke anyway, and the Pantages was bought soon after by a big entertainment company, which asked the Mirvishes to run the theatre. The fax/printer/camera giant Canon, with deep pockets and a big heart, pours in money every year to keep the place running, and now the theatre is called—no surprise—the Canon.

## It's Showtime!

The Toronto theatrical scene is more—much more—than the Mirvishes and their musicals. After New York and London, the city is the third largest live theatre centre in the English-speaking world, with more than 200 professional theatre and dance companies entertaining 7 million people every year.

The offerings meet every taste and budget, from drama, comedy, children's theatre, French-language and First Nations plays to a few done entirely in American Sign Language. Admission prices range from $100 a pop to PWYC ("Pay What You Can"). Shakespeare is performed in the parks in summer; farces fill the seats in old fire halls. Monologues make audiences merry or mute with pity; edgy, experimental stuff sometimes stirs imaginations (and sometimes empties the theatre). Torrid tango competes with street-smart hip hop, and high-class ballet with high-stepping acrobatics. A production can run one night, like a tryout in a church basement, or 25 years, like Agatha Christie's *The Mousetrap*.

In Toronto, every night is opening night.

## Moose in the City

In the summer of 2000, 326 moose appeared on the streets of Toronto. Life-sized, made of fibreglass, painted, decorated, clothed, bejewelled, and bearing props that matched their location, they turned Toronto into "the moose capital of the world," according to Mayor Lastman, who had his own "Mel Moose" down at City Hall. A moose with a cast on its leg stood—shakily—in front of Sick Kids Hospital. A dragon moose found a spot in Chinatown. "Rembrandtler Moose"—with beret and paintbrush—adorned the entrance to the Art Gallery. The moose were weird and wonderful. They were funny, too. People noticed. People laughed. People came from far away to see them. (People also swiped their antlers. When the city offered a reward for information on the thefts, even more antlers disappeared.)

All the moose had names. These names were weird and wonderful too: Anonymoose, Chocolate Moose, City Moose and Country Moose, Driving Moose Daisy, Moose Trap, Moosician, Pokemoose, Moosepaper, Wolfgang Amadeus Moozart, and Is That Your Final Antler?

At the end of the months-long event, Moose in the City had brought 2 million tourists and $400 million to Toronto. In 2001 all the moose were auctioned off, and $5 million went to charity and to Olympic athletes. Nevertheless, moose still pop up all over town—and people still laugh.

**Popular "bay and gable" house with frustrated feline**

## Last Words

The old Huron word *To'ron'to* is often said to mean "a place of meeting," but it can also suggest "a gateway," "a land of plenty," and "a place of many people." Throughout its centuries of history Toronto has been all of those things, and it still is. It's a gateway to a better life for those who come from distant countries. It's certainly a land of plenty: a walk through a shopping centre, or St. Lawrence Market (which started selling stuff in 1803, making it Canada's oldest mall), or any of the hundred boutiques in Yorkville is proof enough of the city's wealth. There are more things to eat, to wear, to drive, to own, to buy than anyone could wish for in a thousand lifetimes. And it's a place of many people (and more all the time), most of whom, most of the time, live together in peace.

There are problems, of course. They are the problems of any large, growing, multicultural city. There is still too much poverty, too much garbage, too much traffic. The roads frequently look like parking lots and the air smells like a gas station. There is sometimes hurtful bigotry and ignorant racism. These are grave challenges, challenges that must be met. And the people of Toronto will meet them, as they have throughout their history.

From John Strachan to John Sewell, Elizabeth Stong to Elizabeth McMaster, Edward Lennox to Ed Mirvish, from the kids of Philippe De Grassi to the "Kids of DeGrassi Street," from the Germans who carved Yonge Street out of the forest to the Italians who carved a subway underneath it, from its first citizens to its last, the abiding strength of Toronto has always been its people, working as a team. Together, they overcame war, rebellion, plague, fire, and flood—and sometimes their own leaders—to build a great city. Together, they now look forward to a future in which their great city can be greater still.

# Timelines

**BC**

| | |
|---|---|
| 40,000 to 15,000 | People travel from Asia to North America over the land bridge connecting them. |
| 11,000 | The glaciers shrink, melt, claw out the Great Lakes. |
| 10,000 | More than half the large mammals in North America vanish, including the mastodon, the hairy mammoth, the sabre-toothed cat, the lion, the horse, the dire wolf, the giant dog, the woolly rhinoceros, and the cave bear. |
| 9500 | People come to the north shore of Lake Ontario. |
| 2675 | First Egyptian mummy. |
| 2500 | The Chinese invent ink. |
| 1800 | The Stonehenge rocks are rolled into place. |
| 776 | First Olympic Games. |
| 214 | The Great Wall of China, eventually 2,400 kilometres (1,500 miles) long and 9 metres (10 yards) high, is begun. |
| 150 | The Chinese invent paper. |

**AD**

| | |
|---|---|
| 500 | The Huron set up camps near the Humber. |
| 594 | Bubonic plague kills half the people in Europe. |
| 704 | The Chinese invent movable type. |
| 1000 | Vikings land in Newfoundland. |
| 1350 | Bubonic plague kills three-quarters of the people in Europe. |
| 1455 | Johann Gutenberg reinvents movable type. |
| 1492 | Columbus sets out for China and bumps into North America. |
| 1497 | Giovanni Caboto, a.k.a. John Cabot, puts an English flag on Cape Breton, or maybe Newfoundland, or possibly Labrador. |
| 1500 or so | The Huron move north to Lake Simcoe and Georgian Bay, probably to get away from the imperialistic Iroquois. |

| | |
|---|---|
| 1534-5 | Cartier cruises up a river and calls it the St. Lawrence. |
| 1608-10 | Champlain explores, draws maps, and founds Quebec. |
| 1615 | Étienne Brûlé is the first European to set foot on Toronto soil. |
| 1629 | An African boy, later named Oliver, is the first human being sold as a slave in Canada. |
| 1640 | The Huron catch smallpox from the Europeans. Half of them die. |
| 1667 | Canada's first census counts 3,215 people – but none of them is Native. |
| 1720 | France builds a trading post at Toronto to handle the booming beaver business. |
| 1750 | France builds a bigger trading post and calls it Fort Rouillé. Everybody else calls it Fort Toronto. |
| 1756 | Britain and France have a war about European real estate and North American fur. |
| 1759 | France torches Fort Toronto so the Brits can't use it. |
| 1763 | The Brits win the war. |
| 1770 | Jean Baptiste Rousseau, who later guides the Simcoes into Toronto bay, builds a house on the Humber. |
| 1776 | Thirteen British colonies declare independence and war, then turn themselves into the United States of America. |
| 1788 | England buys the Toronto region – about 260,000 acres – from the Mississauga. |
| 1789 | France has a revolution. |
| 1791 | Upper Canada is set up as a separate British colony. The Simcoes come to Niagara to run it. |
| 1793 | The Simcoes move to Toronto, camp out in a tent, and change the name to York. |
| 1794 | William and Charlotte Berczy land at the mouth of the Don with five dozen German families, who build half the new town and settle Markham. |

| | |
|---|---|
| 1800 | Hogs are no longer allowed to run free in York. |
| 1807 | The first church and the first public school open in York. |
| 1812 | John Strachan rides into town and takes over as head of the church, head of the school, and head of everything else. |
| 1813-14 | A European war comes to North America. United States and Canada shoot at each other. Many die. Nobody wins. |
| 1817 | A regular stagecoach churns up the mud between York and Kingston. |
| 1825 | William Lyon Mackenzie comes to York and changes history. |
| 1826 | Steamboats and most of Mackenzie's type appear in the bay. |
| 1832 | Cholera kills 237 people in York. Town printers form a union; it's still going strong. |
| 1834 | The town of York becomes the city of Toronto. Mackenzie is made mayor. Slavery is abolished in the British Empire. |
| 1835 | Toronto's first garbage collector, called a scavenger, starts collecting. |
| 1837 | Mackenzie leads a rebellion against the Family Compact. |
| 1838 | The rebellion is crushed and some leaders are hanged. Hanged too is Julia Murdoch, the first woman sentenced to death in Toronto, after she poisons her boss and steals the silver. |
| 1841 | Upper and Lower Canada are united. Toronto is all aglow with its first gas lamps. |
| 1843 | King's College – later the U of T – enrolls its first student. |
| 1848 | Responsible government comes to Upper Canada. Egerton Ryerson abolishes school fees and all 15 Toronto schools close for a year. |
| 1849 | First Great Fire destroys the downtown core. |
| 1851 | Toronto gets its first railway. Canada gets its first postage stamp. |
| 1858 | A big storm carves out Toronto Island. |
| 1861 | Yonge gets its first streetcar tracks for horse-drawn trolleys. |
| 1867 | Canada is born. So is Ontario, and Toronto is its capital. John Strachan dies. |
| 1869 | A young Irish storekeeper named Timothy Eaton sets up shop at Queen and Yonge. |
| 1871 | Children in Ontario must attend school: it's the law. |
| 1875 | Elizabeth McMaster opens an 11-room hospital, which grows up to be the Hospital for Sick Children. Toronto's Henry Woodward takes out a patent on the first electric light bulb. |
| 1876 | Alexander Graham Bell makes the first phone call. |
| 1877 | A roller rink opens at St. Lawrence Hall. Tickets are 25 cents. Skates are free. |
| 1878 | The Ex – the biggest show on earth – opens its gates. |
| 1882 | The Ex is a blaze of glory: 200 electric arc lamps turn night into day. Soon all of downtown Toronto lights up. |
| 1883 | Augusta Stowe-Gullen is the first woman to teach at Toronto Women's Medical College. Ada Marean opens Canada's first kindergarten at Louisa Street School. North America's first electric streetcar is shown off at the Ex. |
| 1884 | Toronto Public Library lends its first book. |
| 1893 | Governor General Stanley gives a $50 silver cup, now the oldest sports trophy in North America, to Montreal AAA hockey team. |

| | |
|---|---|
| 1894 | Arthur Conan Doyle reads a Sherlock Holmes story at Massey Hall. Toronto is the first city in Canada to mark Labour Day. |
| 1899 | A new City Hall, to serve Toronto's 200,000 people, opens for business at Bay and Queen. |
| 1900 | Cars run all over the roads and into each other. William Christie, who made good cookies, dies. |
| 1904 | Second Great Fire makes charcoal of downtown T.O. Wood is banned for city buildings. Henry Pellatt buys stones from Scotland and starts his house on the hill – Casa Loma. |
| 1905 | Santa Claus first comes to town. |
| 1906 | Tom Longboat beats a horse in a 12-mile race, then beats the world in a marathon. |
| 1907 | The Royal Alex issues its first theatre ticket and Toronto issues its first parking ticket. Tobogganing on Sunday is a crime. |
| 1908 | Thousands throng Scarborough Beach to see an airplane. |
| 1909 | U of T football team wins the first Grey Cup. |
| 1914 | Henry finishes his house, the ROM and the Winter Garden Theatre open, Toronto wins its first Stanley Cup, World War I starts – and the last passenger pigeon on earth dies. |
| 1917 | Women get the vote. The Viaduct over the Don River Valley joins Danforth and Bloor. |
| 1918 | World War I ends. |
| 1919 | E.P. Taylor patents an electric toaster that browns both sides of a slice of bread at the same time, and earns his first dollar. |
| 1920 | The first Canadian commercial radio programs are aired. Constance Hamilton is first woman elected to Toronto city council. The Pantages Theatre opens. |
| 1922 | Banting and Macleod get the Nobel Prize for discovering insulin. Canadian Tire opens first store. |
| 1923 | Foster Hewitt does the first hockey play-by-play from Mutual Street Arena. |
| 1927 | Toronto swimmer George Young, 17, wins the Wrigley Marathon. |
| 1928 | The first movie cartoon with sound is shown. |
| 1929 | The British Privy Council says women are persons. The Great Depression sets in and stays around for 10 years. |
| 1930 | The tape recorder is invented. Claire Mackay is born at 291 Roncesvalles Avenue in Toronto's west end. |
| 1931 | Maple Leaf Gardens is built. The 34-storey Bank of Commerce opens, tallest building in British Empire. Mickey and Prince, the last two horses in the Toronto Fire Department, are put out to pasture. |
| 1933 | Adolf Hitler takes over Germany. |
| 1939 | King George and Queen Elizabeth come to Toronto. First flight out of the new airport at Malton: Toronto to Vancouver for $225, at 201 m.p.h. World War II starts. |
| 1942 | Twenty thousand Japanese Canadians are put in prison camps in British Columbia. |
| 1944 | At the first Kiwanis music festival, a 10-year-old pianist named Glenn Gould is the winner. The worst snowstorm in Toronto's history stops the city for three days. |
| 1945 | World War II ends. Mothers get their first family allowance cheques. |
| 1948 | Honest Ed's discount store opens at Bloor and Bathurst. |
| 1949 | A century after the First Great Fire, the steamship *Noronic* burns in Toronto harbour, killing 118. |

| 1950 | Shoppers greet the credit card. Sunday sports are legal. |
| 1953 | Twelve cities join Toronto to make Metro. Johnny Wales is born in Toronto. |
| 1954 | Canada's first subway is built under Yonge Street. Marilyn Bell, 16, is first person to swim Lake Ontario. Hurricane Hazel kills 81 in Toronto. |
| 1957 | Toronto radio station CHUM goes to rock 'n' roll. Russian satellite *Sputnik* launches the space age. |
| 1959 | The St. Lawrence Seaway opens. The microchip starts a revolution that is still going on. |
| 1960 | The last steam locomotive puffs out of Union Station. |
| 1962 | A double hanging at Don Jail marks the last executions in Canada. |
| 1964 | Yorkdale, Canada's first suburban plaza, opens its cash registers. |
| 1965 | As fuddyduds fume, Toronto's daring new City Hall rises at Queen and Bay. Canada gets a new flag. |
| 1966 | Bloor-Danforth subway opens. CBC broadcasts its first colour TV show. |
| 1967 | Canada is 100 years old. |
| 1969 | Earthlings land on the moon. Toronto proclaims first Monday in August as Simcoe Day. |
| 1970 | TVO, Ontario's public service channel, begins broadcasting. |
| 1974 | Metro Zoo is open to the public. U of T's Massey College is open to women. |
| 1976 | The CN Tower is built, the tallest free-standing structure in the world. Eaton's catalogue fills its last mail order. |
| 1980 | "O Canada" becomes the national anthem. |
| 1989 | With a million tons a year, Toronto wins honours as the world's top garbage producer. The SkyDome opens. |

| 1990 | *The Toronto Story* is published by Annick Press to celebrate its 15 years in children's books, and to salute the city as it nears its 200th year as a permanent community. |
| 1991 | The browser and the juice box are invented. Toronto elects its first woman mayor, June Rowlands. |
| 1993 | 200th anniversary of Fort York. |
| 1994 | Major league baseball players go on strike; World Series cancelled. |
| 1997 | Harry Potter is born. |
| 1998 | Canada's worst ice storm: 1,000 transmission towers and 30,000 utility poles are toppled; 100,000 people are forced from their homes. The megacity of Toronto is created by the merger of six separate municipalities. |
| 2000 | More than 400 million people log on to the Internet. |

# More Stories to Read

Bilson, Geoffrey. *Death Over Montreal.* Kids Can Press, 1982. The cholera epidemic of the 1830s.

—— *Hockeybat Harris.* Kids Can Press, 1984. A boy from England is a "war guest" in Canada during World War II.

Bradford, Karleen. *The Other Elizabeth.* Gage (Jeanpac Series), 1982. A girl travels through time to the War of 1812.

Brandeis, Marianne. *The Tinder-box.* Porcupine's Quill, 1982. Family life in southern Ontario, near York, in the 1830s.

—— *The Quarter-Pie Window.* Porcupine's Quill, 1985. An orphaned brother and sister find jobs in York in the 1830s. Sequel to *The Tinder-box.*

Connor, Ralph. *Glengarry School Days.* McClelland and Stewart, New Canadian Library Series, 1975. School days in the Ontario of the 1880s.

Freeman, Bill. *Harbour Thieves.* James Lorimer & Co., 1984. Two children sell newspapers in 1870s Toronto.

Greenwood, Barbara. *A Question of Loyalty.* Scholastic, 1984. The rebellion of 1837, and how it divided families and friends.

Hughes, Monica. *Blaine's Way.* Irwin, 1986. A boy grows up in Ontario during the Dirty Thirties.

Hunter, Bernice Thurman. *That Scatterbrain Booky.* Scholastic, 1981. The first in the series about Booky, a girl who lives in Toronto during the Depression of the 1930s.

—— *With Love From Booky.* Scholastic, 1983. The second in the Booky series.

—— *As Ever, Booky.* Scholastic, 1985. The third in the Booky series.

—— *Lamplighter.* Scholastic, 1987. Life in Muskoka and Toronto in the 1880s.

Kogawa, Joy. *Naomi's Road.* Oxford University Press, 1986. The story of a Japanese Canadian girl and her internment in B.C. during World War II.

McLean, Dirk. *Steel Drums and Ice Skates.* Groundwood Books, 1996. Holly leaves her Trinidad home to join her parents in Toronto, but life in the big city is confusing and difficult.

Oberman, Sheldon. *The White Stone in the Castle Wall.* Tundra, 1996. Why is there one white stone in the wall around Toronto's castle? A story of how it might have happened.

Pearson, Kit. *The Guests of War Trilogy.* Penguin Books, 1998. The story of two English children sent to Toronto during World War II, told in three volumes: *The Sky is Falling, Looking at the Moon,* and *The Lights Go On Again.*

Philip, Marlene Nourbese. *Harriet's Daughter.* Women's Press, 1988. A 13-year-old black girl is at odds with her father in this novel set in west central Toronto in the 1980s.

Reaney, James. *The Boy with an "R" in his Hand.* Porcupine's Quill, 1984 (rev. ed.). The "Type Riot" of 1826.

Sadiq, Nazneen. *Camels Can Make You Homesick.* James Lorimer & Co., 1985. A collection of stories about South Asian immigrant children in modern Toronto.

—— *Heartbreak High.* James Lorimer & Co., 1988. The romance of a Jewish girl and a Muslim boy is threatened by the prejudices of their parents.

Sass, Gregory. *Redcoat.* Porcupine's Quill, 1985. A runaway boy gets caught up in the War of 1812.

Sutherland, Robert. *Son of the Hounds.* Scholastic, 1988. An adventure story set in the War of 1812.

Takashima, Shizuye. *A Child in Prison Camp.* Tundra, 1971. A picture book about a Japanese Canadian child's experience in an internment camp during World War II.

—— *A Child in Prison Camp.* Tundra, 1989. A new edition, with 102 pages of text, suitable for older readers.

Toten, Teresa. *The Onlyhouse.* Red Deer College Press, 1995. Moving into an "onlyhouse"—a single detached home in Toronto—is a dream come true for Lucy and her Croatian mother, but will they ever fit in?

Turner, D. Harold. *Rebel Run.* Gage (Jeanpac Series), 1989. (Formerly *To Hang a Rebel*, Gage, 1977.) A story about a boy who works for Mackenzie in the Rebellion of 1837.

Wilson, Eric. *The Lost Treasure of Casa Loma.* General Publishing, 1982. Tom and Liz Austen solve a mystery in Toronto's famous castle.

## Other Books You Might Enjoy

Batten, Jack. *The Leafs.* Key Porter Books, 2nd ed., 1999. History, anecdotes, and inside stories of the Toronto Maple Leafs hockey club.

Bolt, Carol. *Cyclone Jack.* Simon & Pierre, 1975. A play about marathon runner Tom Longboat.

Galloway, Priscilla, compiler. *Too Young to Fight: Memories of Our Youth in World War II.* Stoddart Kids, 1999. Contributions by Christopher Chapman and Claire Mackay.

Gould, Allan, and Wise, Leonard. *Toronto Street Names: An Illustrated Guide to their Origins.* Firefly Books, 2000.

Jameson, Anna Brownell. *Winter Studies and Summer Rambles in Canada.* McClelland and Stewart, New Canadian Library Series, 1965. A book about Anna's travels and adventures in Upper Canada from December 1836 to August 1837.

McLean, Dirk. *Play Mas'! A Carnival ABC.* Tundra, 2000. The customs and traditions of the Caribbean Carnival, including the annual celebration in Toronto.

Moak, Allan. *A Big City ABC.* Tundra, 2002 (reissue). An exploration of Toronto in paintings, from baseball to fireworks, from the art gallery to the zoo, from high-rises to High Park.

Simcoe, Elizabeth. *Mrs. Simcoe's Diary.* Mary Quayle Innis, ed. Macmillan, Laurentian Library Series, 1965. A journal of Elizabeth's life in Upper Canada from 1791 to 1796.